ANIMAL ORIGAMI
for the Enthusiast

ANIMAL ORIGAMI
for the Enthusiast

Step-by-Step Instructions in Over 900 Diagrams

25 Original Models by John Montroll

Dover Publications, Inc.
New York

Dedicated to My Parents,
Shirley and Elliott

Published in Canada by General Publishing Company, Ltd., 30 Lesmill Road, Don Mills, Toronto, Ontario.
Published in the United Kingdom by Constable and Company, Ltd.

Animal Origami for the Enthusiast: Step-by-Step Instructions in Over 900 Diagrams is a new work, first published by Dover Publications, Inc., in 1985.

Manufactured in the United States of America
Dover Publications, Inc., 31 East 2nd Street, Mineola, N.Y. 11501

Library of Congress Cataloging in Publication Data

Montroll, John.
   Animal origami for the enthusiast.

   1. Origami.   I. Title.
TT870.M55   1985   736'.982   84-18754
ISBN 0-486-24792-9

INTRODUCTION

The warm reception that greeted *Origami for the Enthusiast* (Dover 23799-0) enables me to present a second collection of original origami projects. I hope that readers take as much delight in folding these designs as I took in concocting them.

Each project in this book is formed by folding a single square sheet of paper. I have adhered to the convention of my first book (and of all my work) in that no sheet is ever cut and no paste or tape is used.

Veteran folders who have not seen my earlier work may find some surprises here. Origami animals often are made without a lot of attention to detail. In particular, the four corners of a square lead quite naturally to three-legged animals. Three of the four corners become legs, and the fourth turns into a head. Since I started folding as a child, I have felt this sort of approximation of shapes to be esthetically unacceptable and technically unnecessary. Much of my research time has gone into developing new folding bases and techniques to make animals that really look like their models. Some of these methods appeared in my first book. Others, in particular the wing-fold, brontosaurus base and five-sided square, appear in print for the first time here. Over the last few years, I have seen many of my techniques enter the mainstream of origami and am proud to contribute to this ancient, elegant art.

Although any square paper can be used for the projects in this book, the best thing to use is standard origami paper. This is sold in many hobby shops, or it can be purchased by mail from the Friends of The Origami Center of America, 15 West 77th Street, New York, N.Y. 10024-5192. Larger sheets of paper are easier to work with than small ones. Origami paper is colored on one side and white on the other. In the diagrams in this book, the shading represents the colored side.

This book uses the international Randlett–Yoshizawa method of notation. Be sure, when folding, to examine not only the step you are on but also the next one, to see the result.

I would like to give special thanks to Eun-Sook Yang for her help with the illustrations.

CONTENTS

SYMBOLS

— — — — — — — —   Valley-fold.

— · · — — · · — — · · —   Mountain-fold.

————————————   Creased-fold. Fold and unfold beforehand; or existing fold.

·   X-ray view or guidelines.

Fold in direction of arrow.

Fold behind.

Unfold.

Fold and unfold.

Push in, sink, squash or reverse-fold.

Turn model over.

Pleat-fold, combination of mountain- and valley-folds.

BASIC FOLDS AND BASES

Pleat-fold

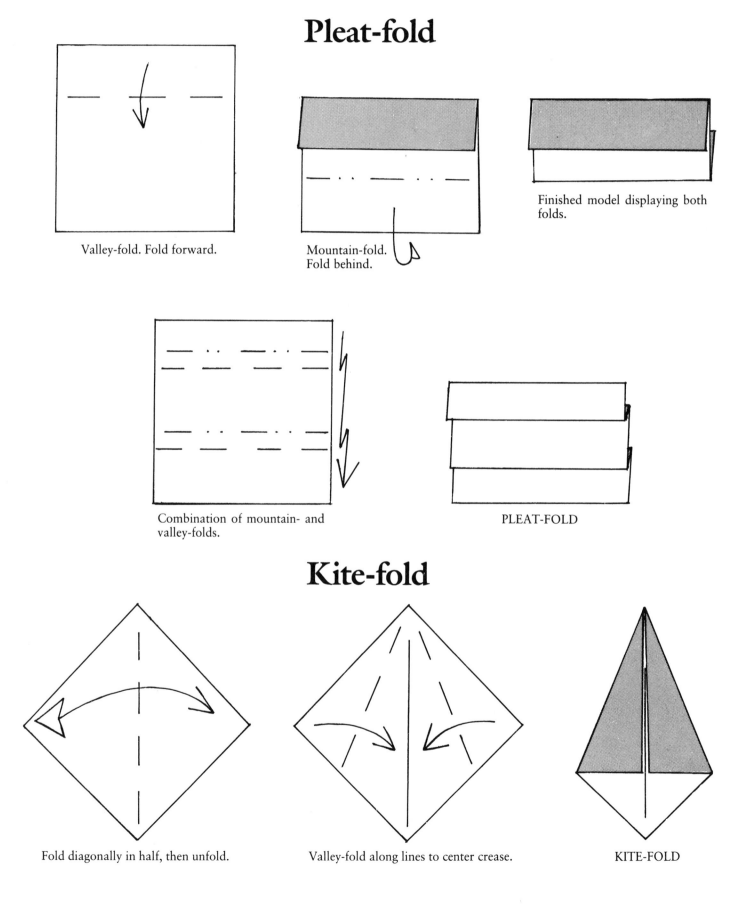

Valley-fold. Fold forward.

Mountain-fold.
Fold behind.

Finished model displaying both
folds.

Combination of mountain- and
valley-folds.

PLEAT-FOLD

Kite-fold

Fold diagonally in half, then unfold.

Valley-fold along lines to center crease.

KITE-FOLD

Reverse- and Crimp-folds

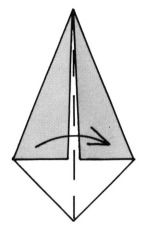

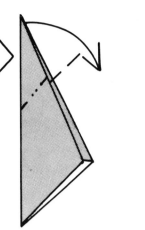

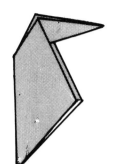

1. To fold all reverse- and crimp-folds begin with kite-fold and fold in half.

2. Fold tip between outer layers. (This fold will appear both ways in future diagrams.)

3. INSIDE REVERSE-FOLD

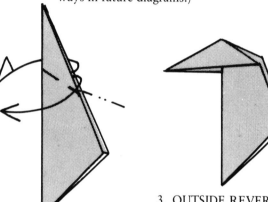

3. OUTSIDE REVERSE-FOLD

2. Open model slightly, then fold tip around outer layers.

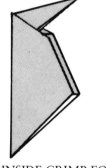

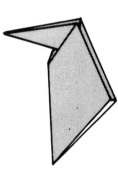

2. Fold behind two reverse-folds, simultaneously.

3. INSIDE CRIMP-FOLD I

2. Fold one reverse-fold to right, then one to left.

3. INSIDE CRIMP-FOLD II

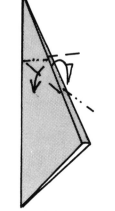

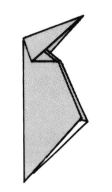

2. Fold one reverse-fold in front and one behind.

3. OUTSIDE CRIMP-FOLD

Rabbit Ear

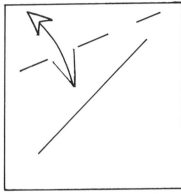

1. Fold and unfold diagonally in half. Fold one side to the center as in a kite-fold and unfold.

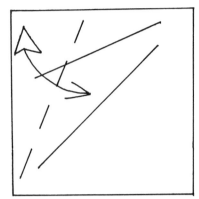

2. Fold and unfold opposite side to the center.

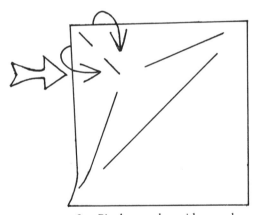

3a. Pinch together sides at the corner and fold down along creases as shown.

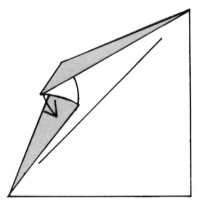

3b. Appearance just before completion.

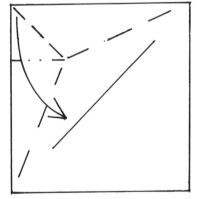

Synopsis of steps 1–3b.

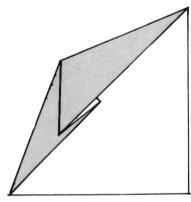

4. RABBIT EAR

Preliminary-fold

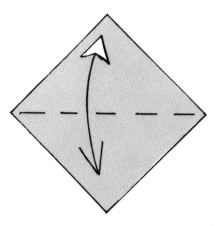

1. Fold diagonally in half, then unfold.

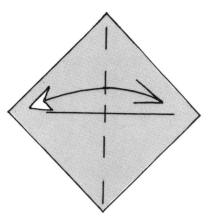

2. Repeat.

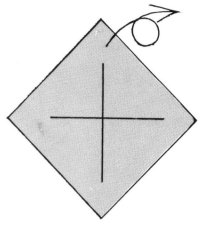

3. Turn over model, then turn clockwise.

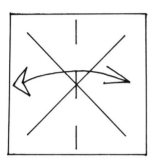

4. Fold in half, then unfold.

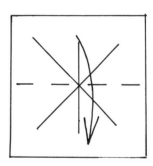

5. Fold in half.

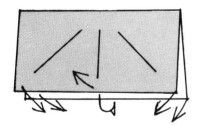

6a. Fold along creases.

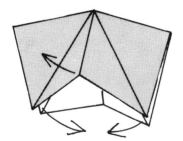

6b. Appearance just before completion.

Synopsis of steps 1–6b.

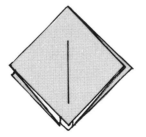

7. PRELIMINARY-FOLD

Petal-fold I

1. Begin with preliminary-fold, then kite-fold.

2. Fold triangular tip down.

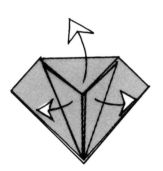

3. Unfold tip, then kite-fold.

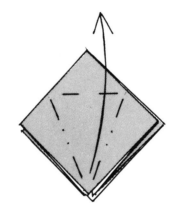

4a. Lift top layer up along creases.

4b. Fold along creases while lifting.

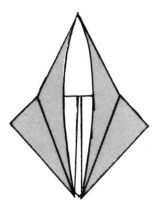

4c. Appearance just before completion.

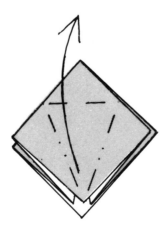

Synopsis of steps 1–4c.

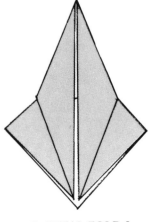

5. PETAL-FOLD I

Bird Base

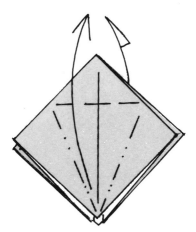

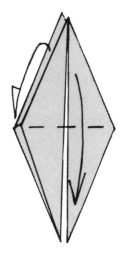

1. Begin with preliminary-fold, then petal-fold both sides.

2. Fold tops of both sides down.

3. BIRD BASE

Squash-fold

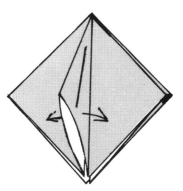

1. Begin with preliminary-fold, then fold and unfold as shown.

2. Lift flap out from sheet.

3. Insert finger inside flap to squash it.

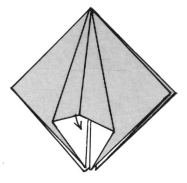

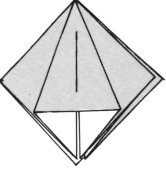

4. Flatten squashed flap.

5. SQUASH-FOLD

Petal-fold II

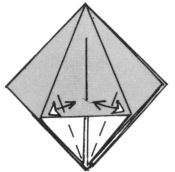

1. Begin with preliminary-fold, squash-fold one layer. Fold and unfold the kite-fold.

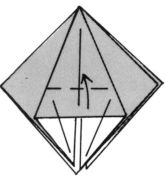

2. Fold edge up into a point.

3. Fold along edges.

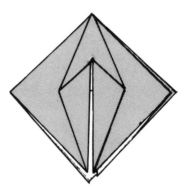

4. PETAL-FOLD II

Double Rabbit Ear

1. Begin with kite-fold, then fold in half.

2. Inside reverse-fold.

3. Fold each flap in half.

4. Fold base of point behind.

5. Reverse-fold. (This step may be omitted to produce this alternate form.)

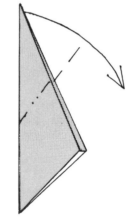

Synopsis of steps 1–5.

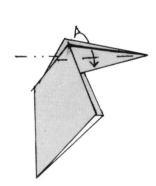

6. DOUBLE RABBIT EAR

Water Bomb Base

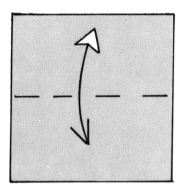

1. Fold horizontally in half, then unfold.

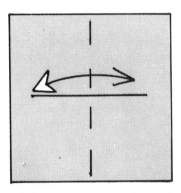

2. Fold vertically in half, then unfold.

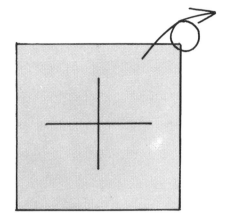

3. Turn model over.

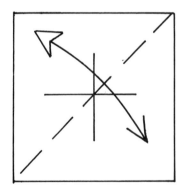

4. Fold diagonally in half, then unfold.

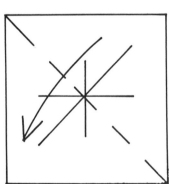

5. Fold diagonally in half along dashed line.

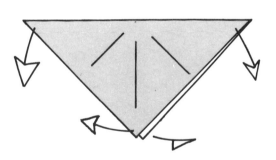

6. Fold along creases (Model will open slightly.)

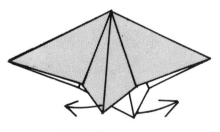

7. Fold along creases.

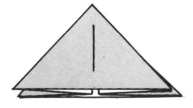

8. WATER BOMB BASE

Brontosaurus Base

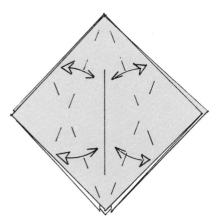

1. Begin with the preliminary-fold.

2.

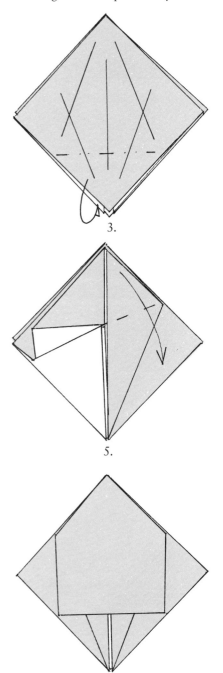

3.

4. Squash-fold.

5.

6. Repeat steps 4 & 5 on the left side.

7. Repeat steps 1–6 behind.

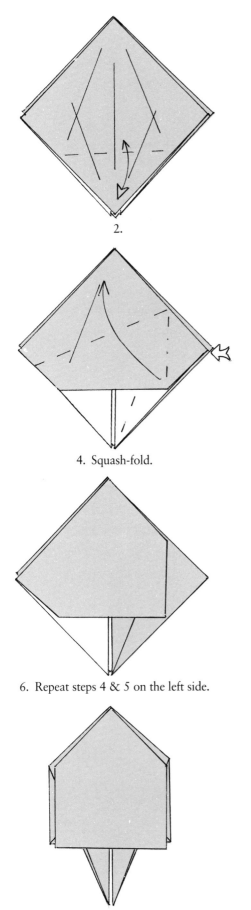

8. BRONTOSAURUS BASE

Wing-fold

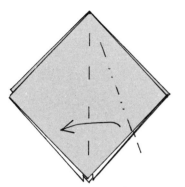

1. Begin with the preliminary-fold. Squash-fold.

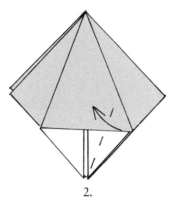

2.

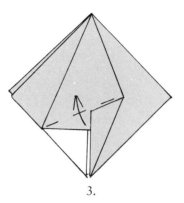

3.

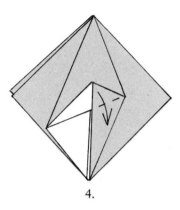

4.

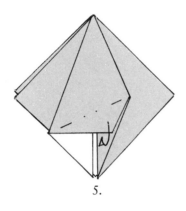

5.

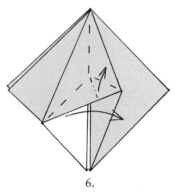

6.

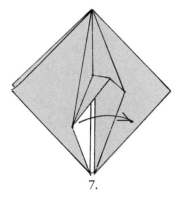

7.

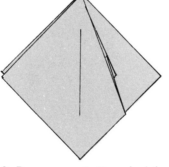

8. Repeat steps 1–7 on the left side.

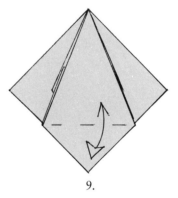

9.

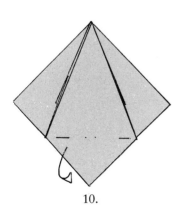

10.

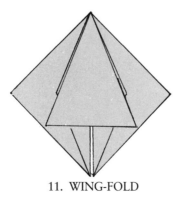

11. WING-FOLD

ANGELFISH

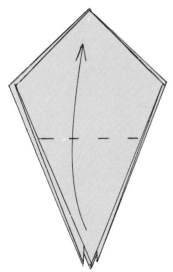

1. Begin with the bird base.

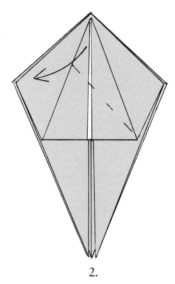

2.

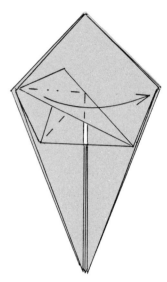

3. Squash-fold.

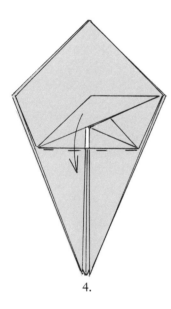

4.

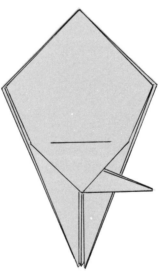

5. Repeat steps 1–4 behind.

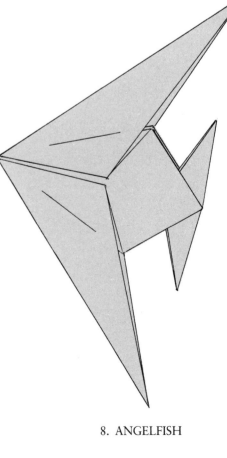

8. ANGELFISH

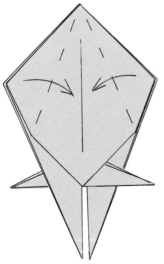

6. Repeat behind.

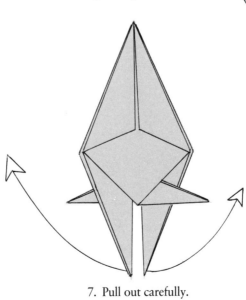

7. Pull out carefully.

SEAL

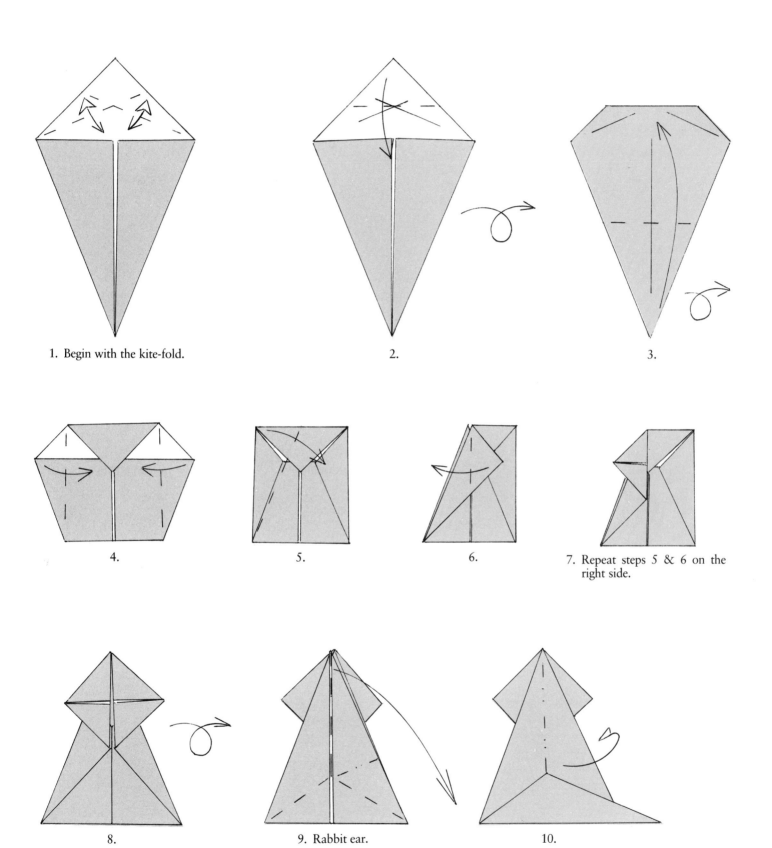

1. Begin with the kite-fold.

2.

3.

4.

5.

6.

7. Repeat steps 5 & 6 on the right side.

8.

9. Rabbit ear.

10.

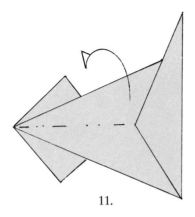

11.

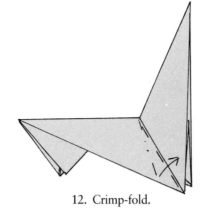

12. Crimp-fold.

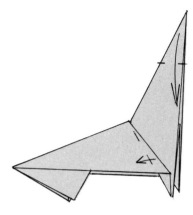

13. Repeat behind.

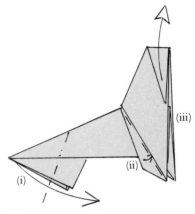

14. (i) Reverse-fold.
    (ii) Tuck inside; repeat behind.
    (iii) Unfold.

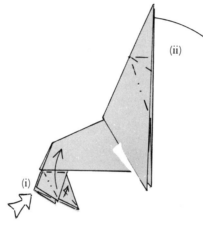

15. (i) Squash-fold; repeat behind.
    (ii) Crimp-fold.

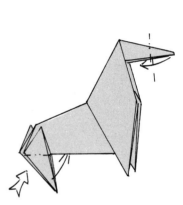

16. Reverse-fold inside the body.

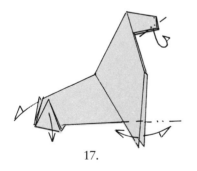

17.

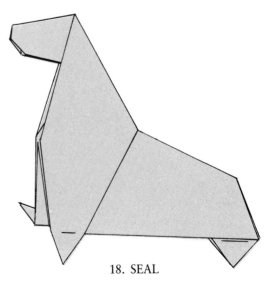

18. SEAL

WALRUS

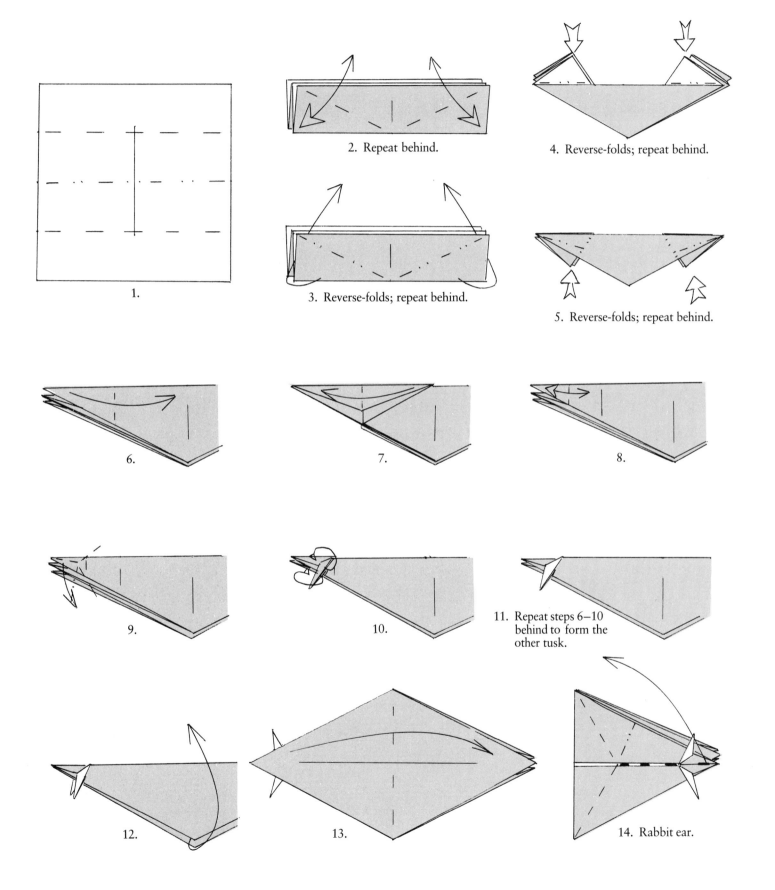

2. Repeat behind.

4. Reverse-folds; repeat behind.

3. Reverse-folds; repeat behind.

5. Reverse-folds; repeat behind.

6.

7.

8.

9.

10.

11. Repeat steps 6–10 behind to form the other tusk.

12.

13.

14. Rabbit ear.

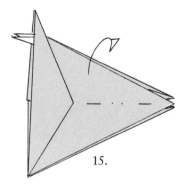

15.

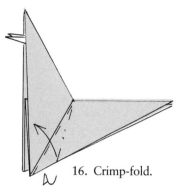

16. Crimp-fold.

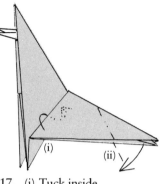

17. (i) Tuck inside.
(ii) Reverse-fold; repeat behind.

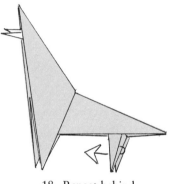

18. Repeat behind.

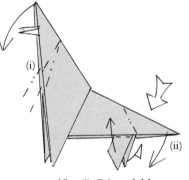

19. (i) Crimp-fold.
(ii) Reverse-fold.

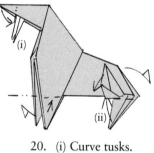

20. (i) Curve tusks.
(ii) Tuck inside.

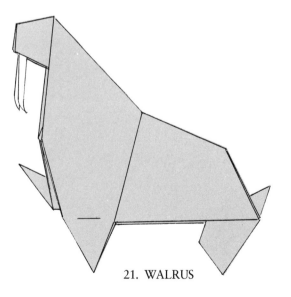

21. WALRUS

STARFISH

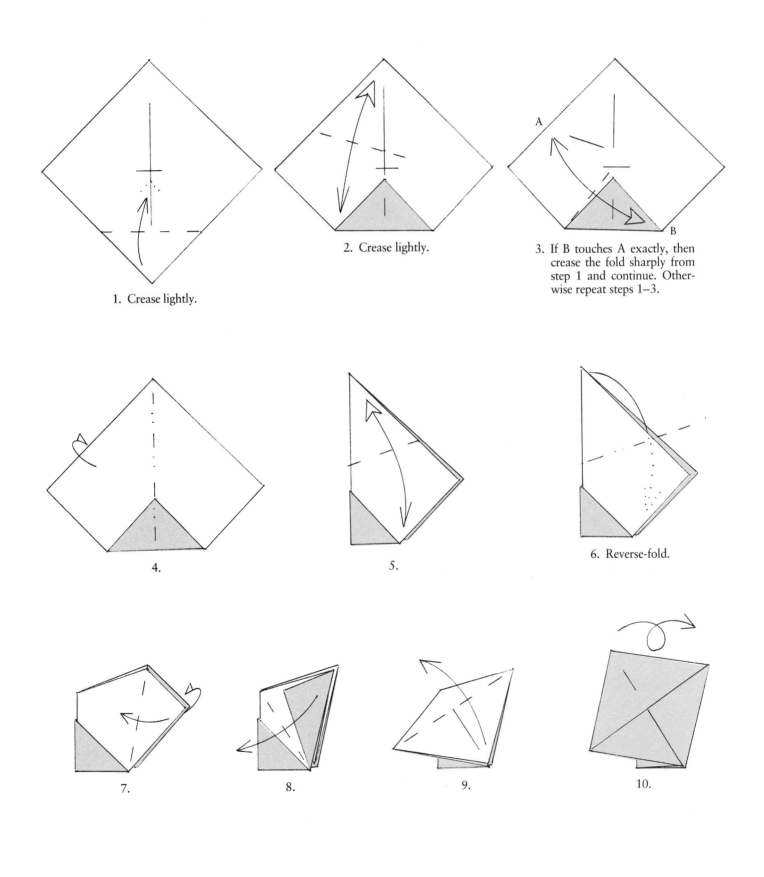

1. Crease lightly.

2. Crease lightly.

3. If B touches A exactly, then crease the fold sharply from step 1 and continue. Otherwise repeat steps 1–3.

4.

5.

6. Reverse-fold.

7.

8.

9.

10.

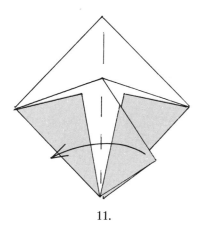

11.

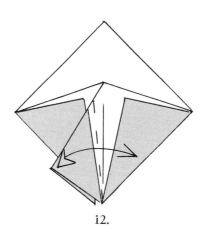

i2.

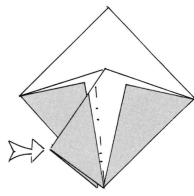

13. Reverse-fold.

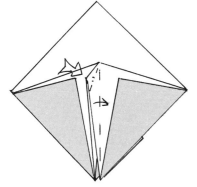

14. Squash-fold.

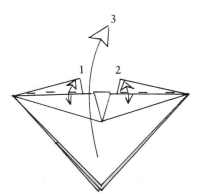

15.

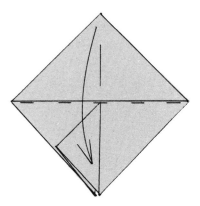

16. FIVE-SIDED SQUARE

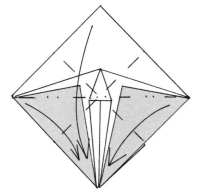

17. (Fold in order)

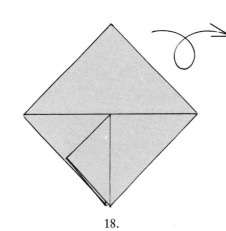

18.

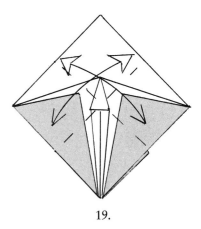

19.

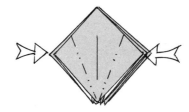

20. Fold the preliminary-fold.

21. FIVE-SIDED PRELIMINARY-FOLD.
Five reverse-folds.

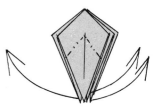

22. FIVE-SIDED BIRD BASE.
Reverse-folds.

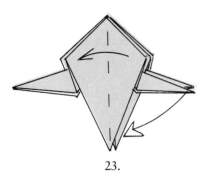

23.

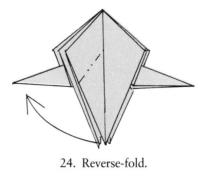

24. Reverse-fold.

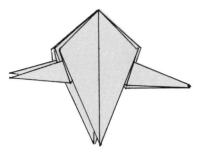

25. Repeat steps 23 & 24 behind.

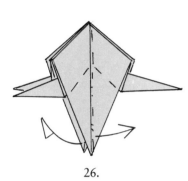

26.

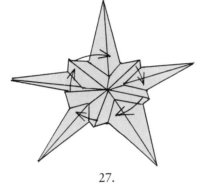

27.

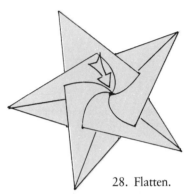

28. Flatten.

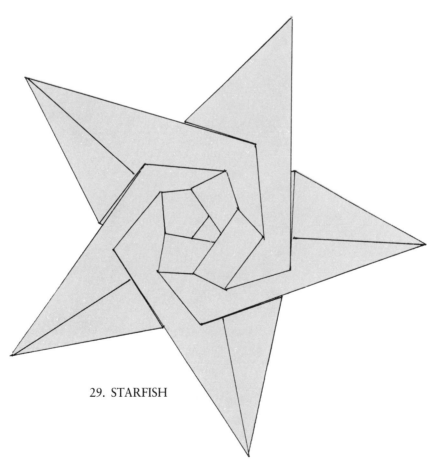

29. STARFISH

CRANE

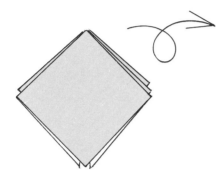

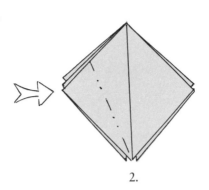

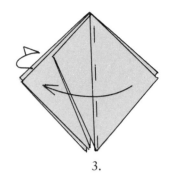

1. Begin with the five-sided preliminary-fold (p. 22).

2.

3.

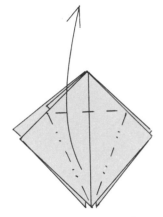

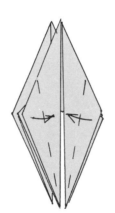

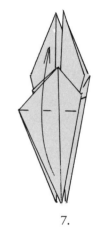

4. Repeat behind.

5. Repeat behind.

6.

7.

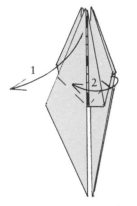

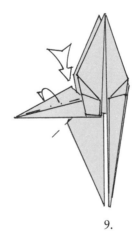

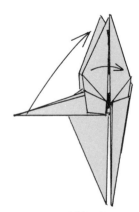

8. (Fold in order)

9.

10. Fold back to step 8.

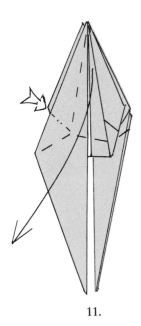

11.

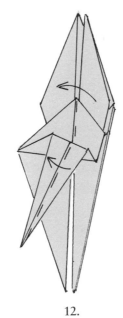

12.

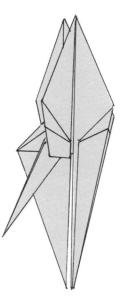

13. Repeat steps 6–12 behind.

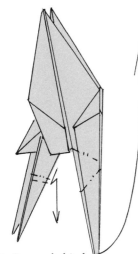

14. Repeat behind.

16. CRANE

15a. (i) Repeat behind.
(ii) Outside reverse-fold.
(iii) Pull wings and flatten body.

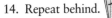

(iii)

(ii)

(i)

(fold in order)

15b. Pull out some paper; repeat behind.

15c. Crimp-fold.

NOTE: Any time there are numbers on a drawing, do the folds in the indicated order.

SWAN

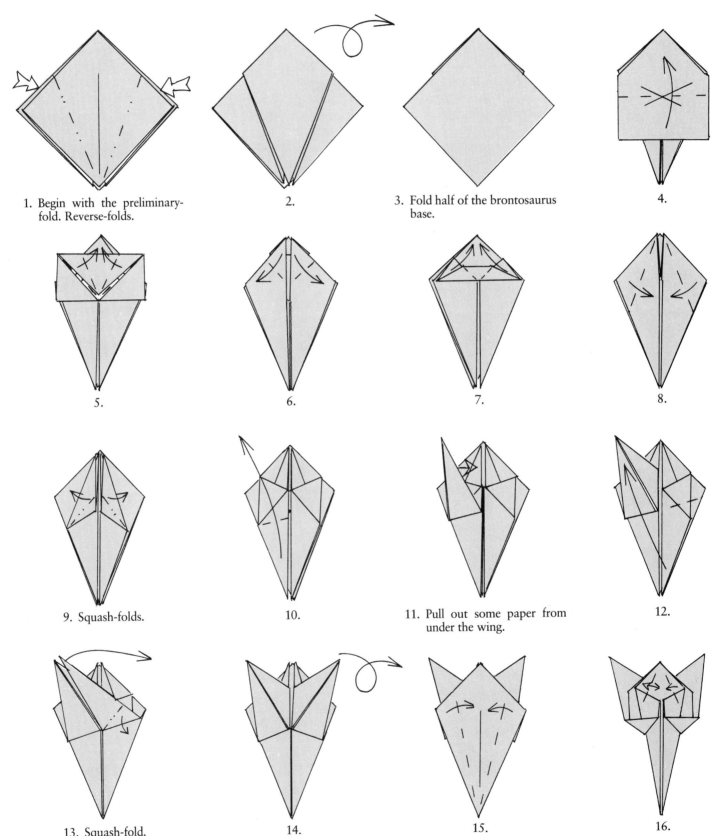

1. Begin with the preliminary-fold. Reverse-folds.

2.

3. Fold half of the brontosaurus base.

4.

5.

6.

7.

8.

9. Squash-folds.

10.

11. Pull out some paper from under the wing.

12.

13. Squash-fold.

14.

15.

16.

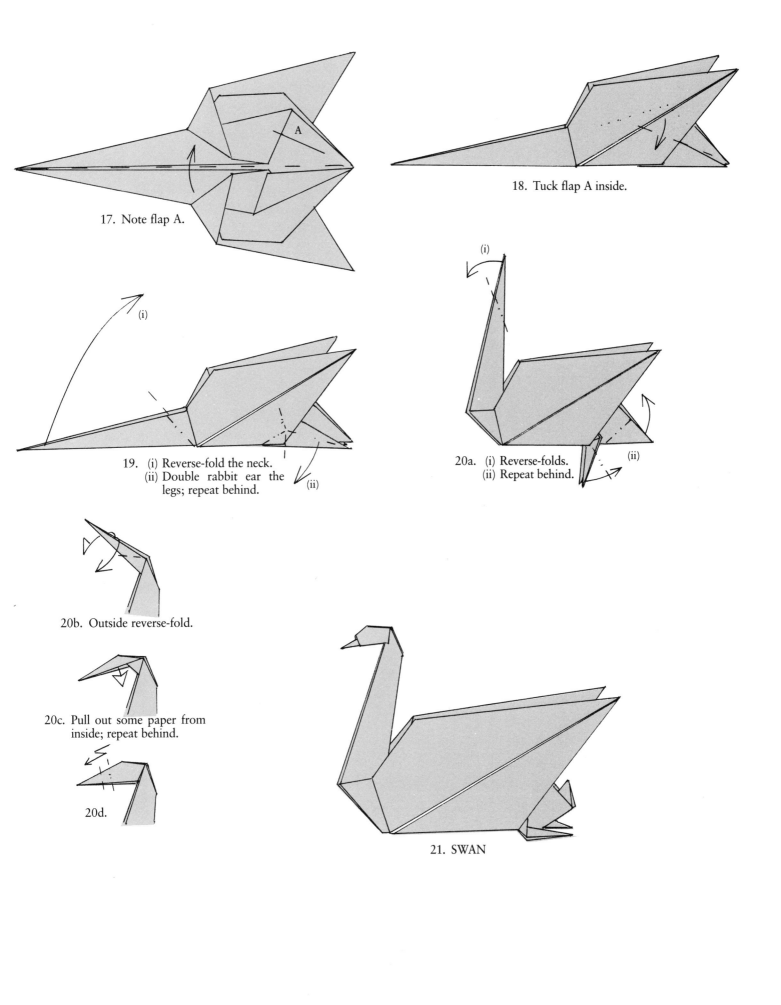

17. Note flap A.

18. Tuck flap A inside.

19. (i) Reverse-fold the neck.
    (ii) Double rabbit ear the legs; repeat behind.

20a. (i) Reverse-folds.
     (ii) Repeat behind.

20b. Outside reverse-fold.

20c. Pull out some paper from inside; repeat behind.

20d.

21. SWAN

EAGLE

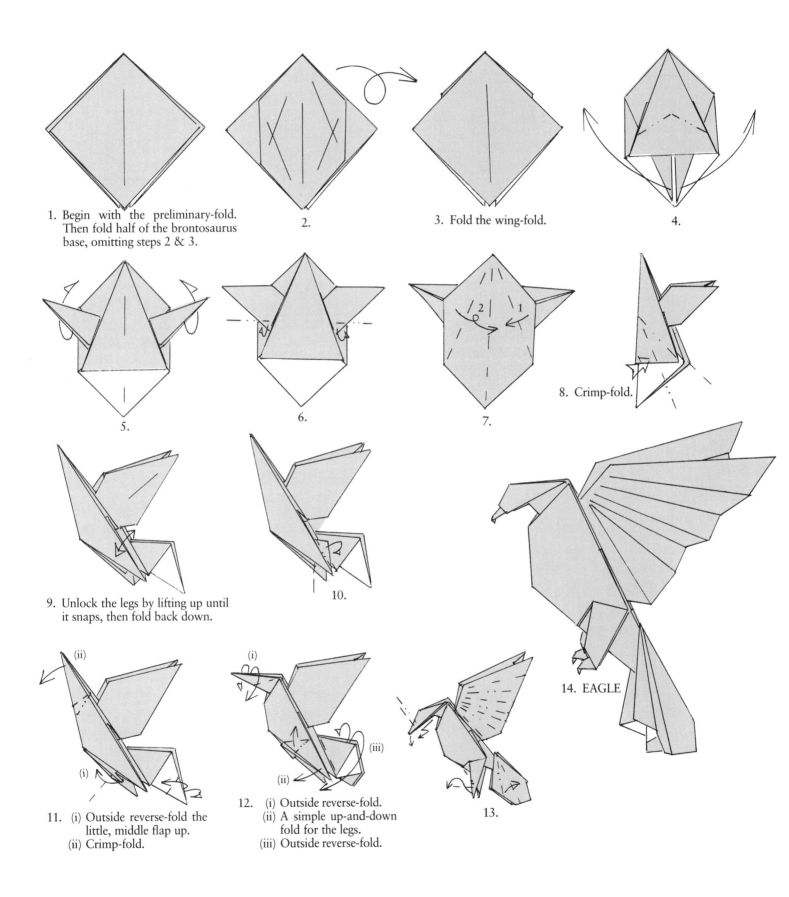

1. Begin with the preliminary-fold. Then fold half of the brontosaurus base, omitting steps 2 & 3.

2.

3. Fold the wing-fold.

4.

5.

6.

7.

8. Crimp-fold.

9. Unlock the legs by lifting up until it snaps, then fold back down.

10.

11. (i) Outside reverse-fold the little, middle flap up.
   (ii) Crimp-fold.

12. (i) Outside reverse-fold.
   (ii) A simple up-and-down fold for the legs.
   (iii) Outside reverse-fold.

13.

14. EAGLE

OWL

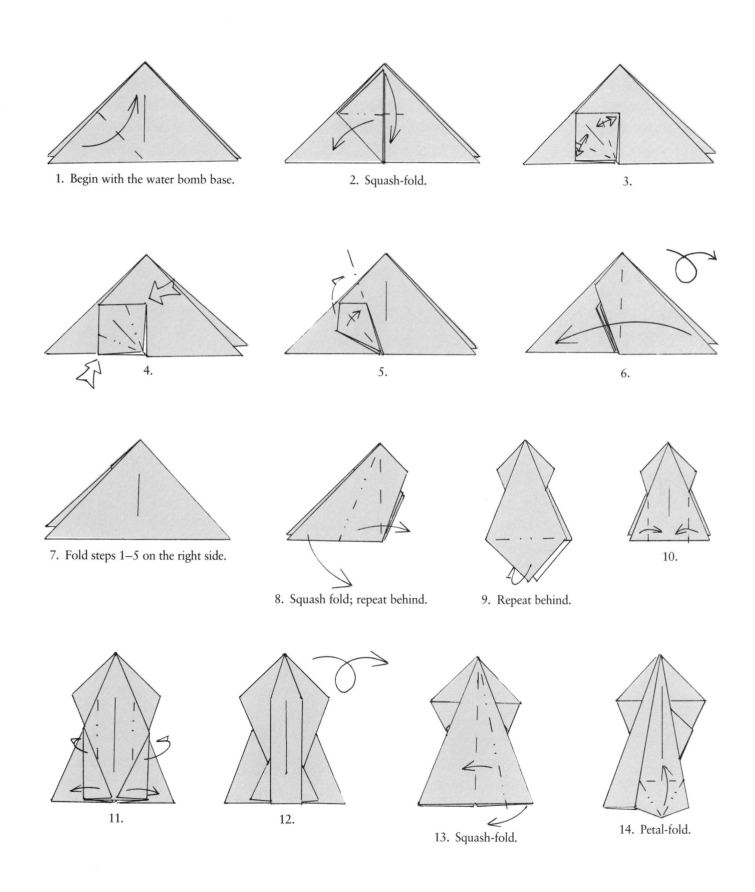

1. Begin with the water bomb base.

2. Squash-fold.

3.

4.

5.

6.

7. Fold steps 1–5 on the right side.

8. Squash fold; repeat behind.

9. Repeat behind.

10.

11.

12.

13. Squash-fold.

14. Petal-fold.

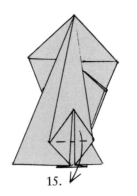

15.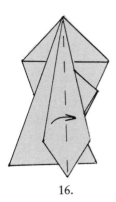

16.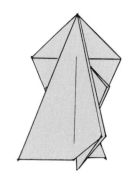

17. Repeat steps 13–16 on the left side.

18.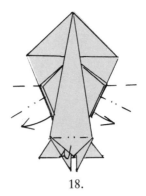

19.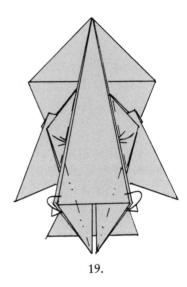

20.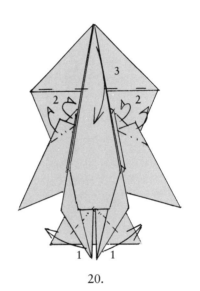

21.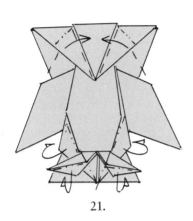

22.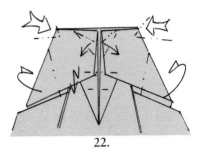

23. OWL

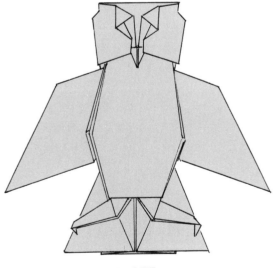

TYRANNOSAURUS

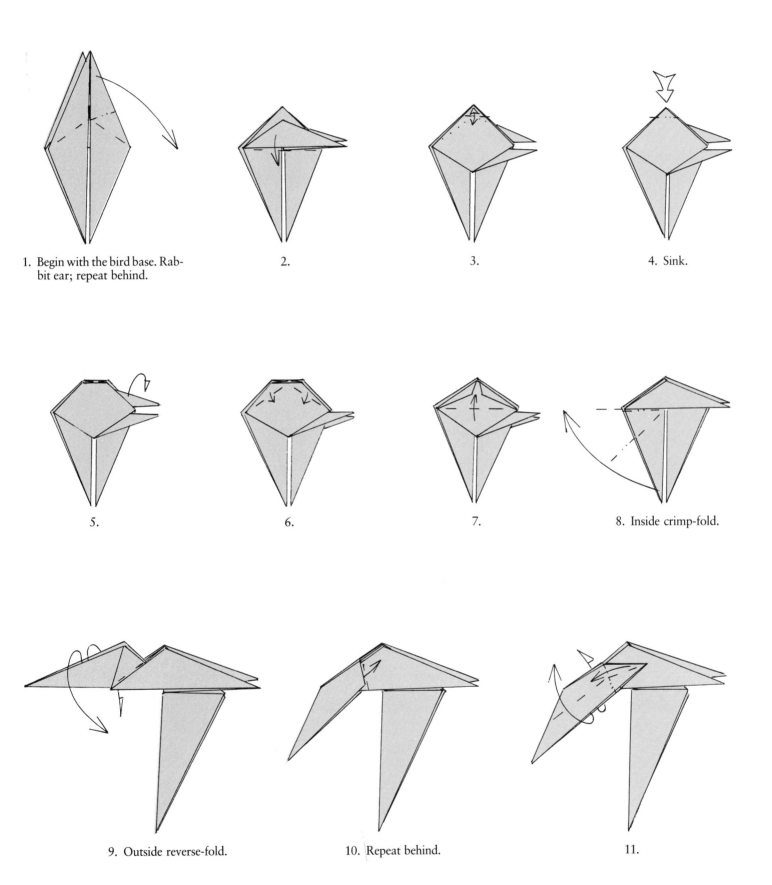

1. Begin with the bird base. Rabbit ear; repeat behind.

2.

3.

4. Sink.

5.

6.

7.

8. Inside crimp-fold.

9. Outside reverse-fold.

10. Repeat behind.

11.

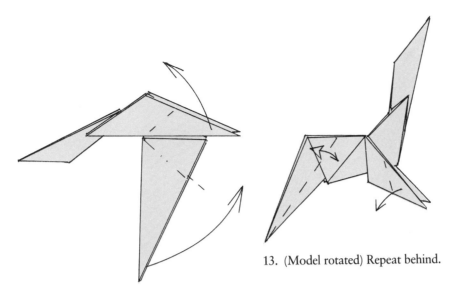

12. Repeat behind.

13. (Model rotated) Repeat behind.

14.

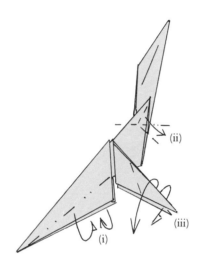

15. (i) Tuck into the center pocket.
(ii) Rabbit ear the arms.
(iii) Outside reverse-fold the legs.

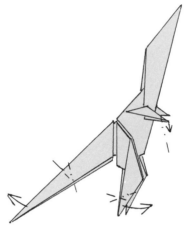

16. Repeat behind.

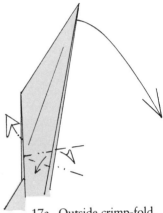

17a. Outside crimp-fold.

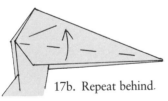

17b. Repeat behind.

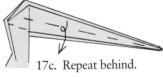

17c. Repeat behind.

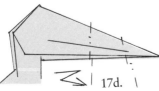

17d.

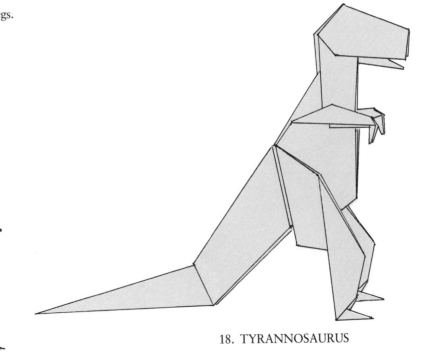

18. TYRANNOSAURUS

BRONTOSAURUS

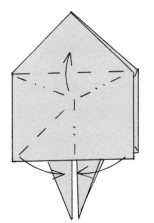

1. Begin with the brontosaurus base; repeat behind.

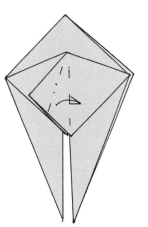

2. Repeat behind.

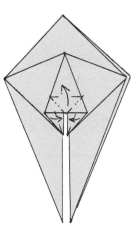

3. Repeat behind.

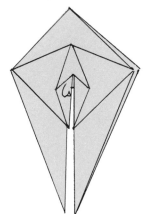

4. Repeat behind.

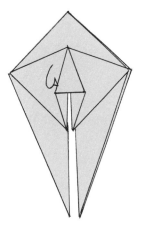

5. Tuck inside; repeat behind.

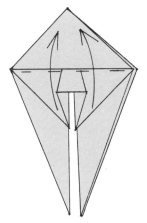

6. Repeat behind.

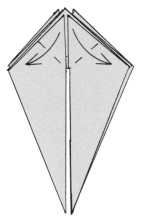

7. Repeat behind.

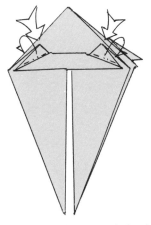

8. Reverse-folds; repeat behind.

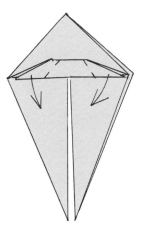

9. Repeat behind.

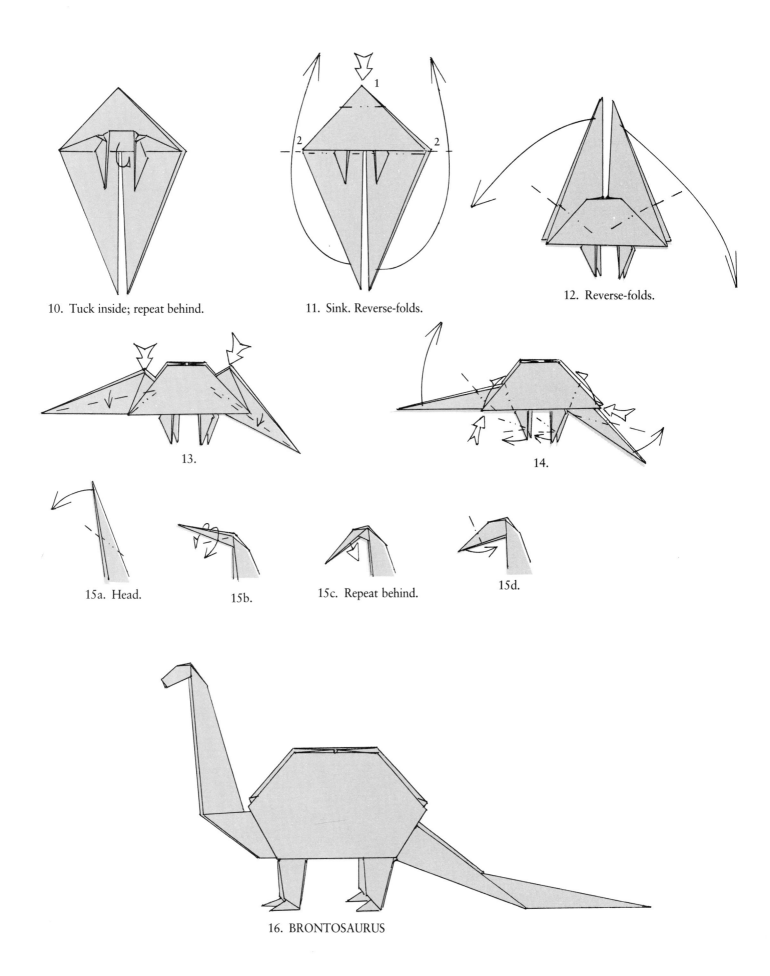

10. Tuck inside; repeat behind.

11. Sink. Reverse-folds.

12. Reverse-folds.

13.

14.

15a. Head.

15b.

15c. Repeat behind.

15d.

16. BRONTOSAURUS

SNAKE

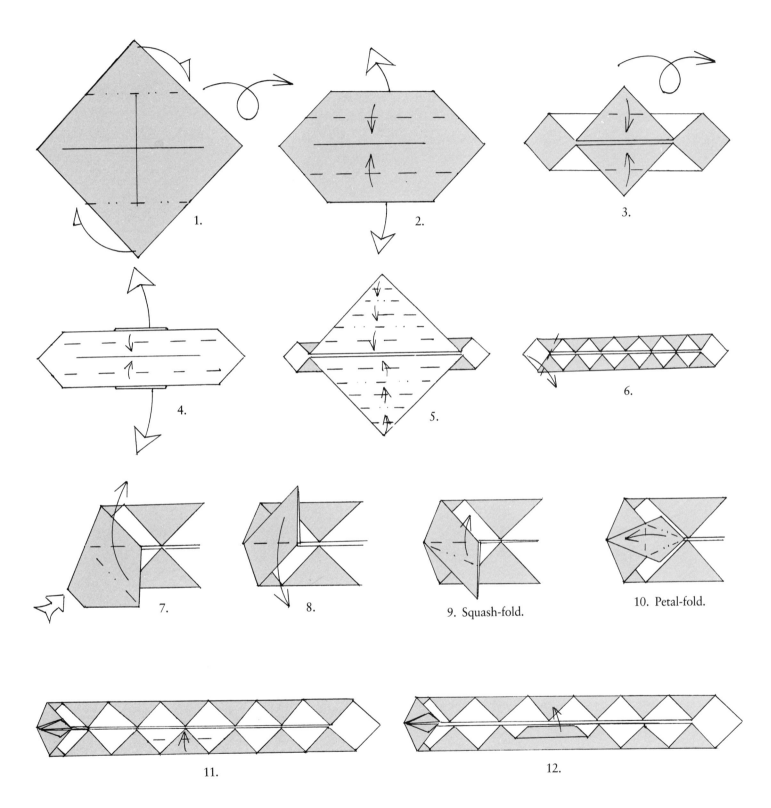

1.

2.

3.

4.

5.

6.

7.

8.

9. Squash-fold.

10. Petal-fold.

11.

12.

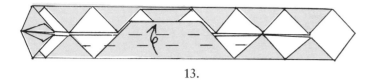

13.

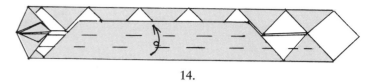

14.

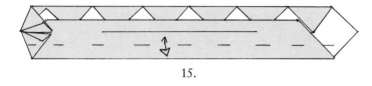

15.

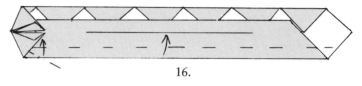

16.

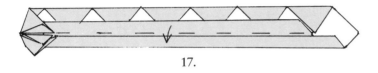

17.

18. Repeat steps 11–17.

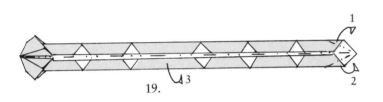

19.

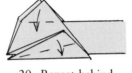

20. Repeat behind.

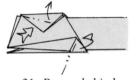

21. Repeat behind.

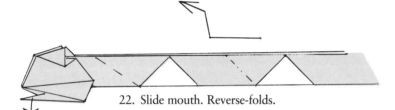

22. Slide mouth. Reverse-folds.

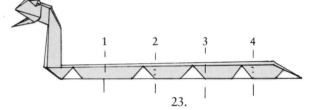

23.

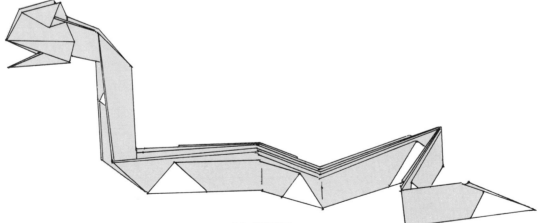

24. SNAKE

TURTLE

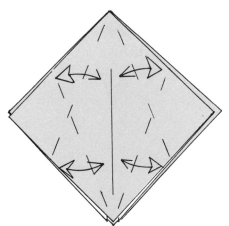

1. Begin with the preliminary-fold; repeat behind.

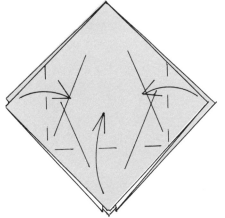

2. Repeat behind.

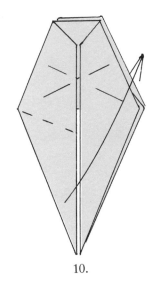

3.

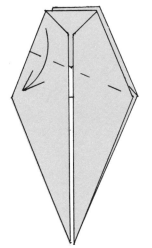

4. Repeat behind.

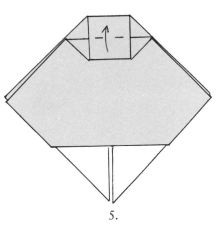

5.

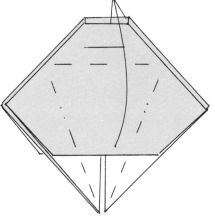

6. Repeat behind.

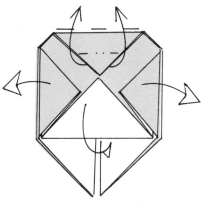

7. Repeat behind.

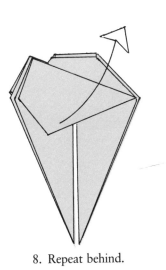

8. Repeat behind.

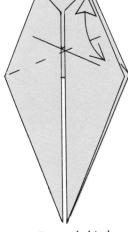

9. Repeat behind.

10.

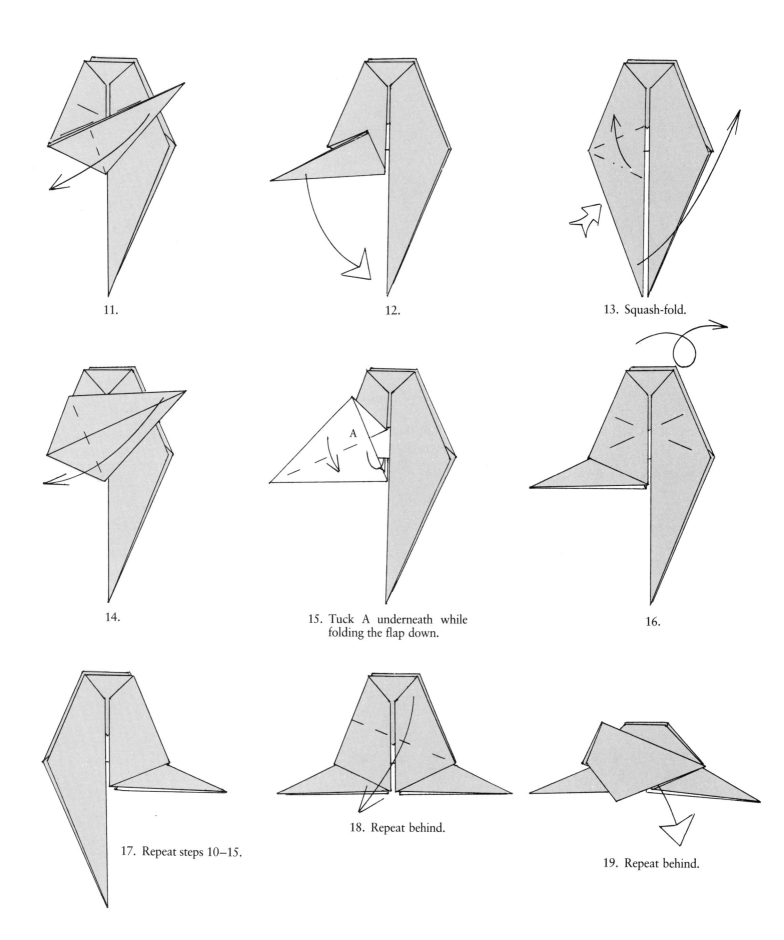

11.

12.

13. Squash-fold.

14.

15. Tuck A underneath while folding the flap down.

16.

17. Repeat steps 10–15.

18. Repeat behind.

19. Repeat behind.

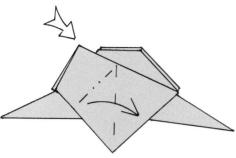

20. Repeat behind.

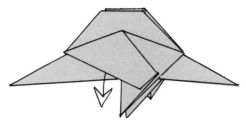

21. Repeat behind.

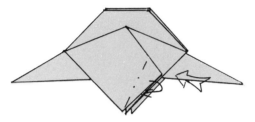

22. Repeat behind.

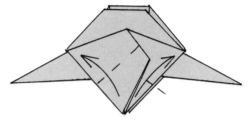

23. Repeat behind.

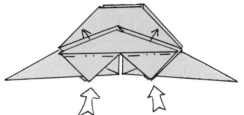

24. Reverse-folds; repeat behind.

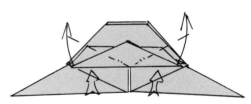

25. Repeat behind.

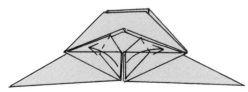

26. Repeat behind.

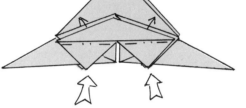

27. Reverse-folds; repeat behind.

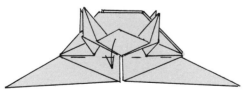

28. Repeat behind.

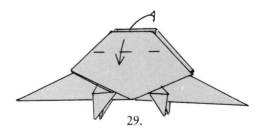

29.

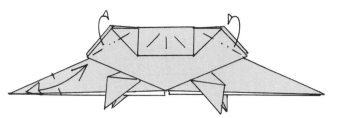

30. Tuck inside; repeat behind.

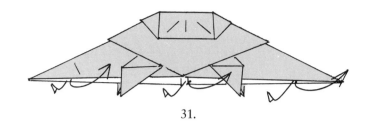

31.

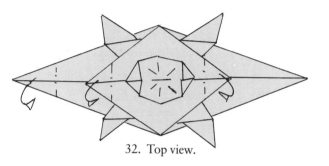

32. Top view.

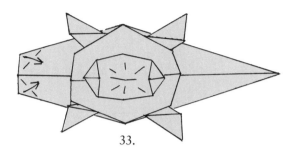

33.

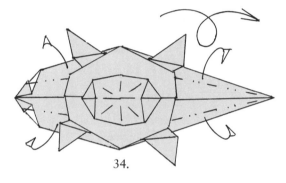

34.

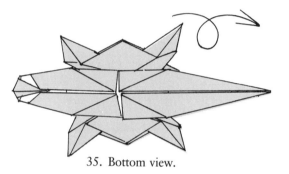

35. Bottom view.

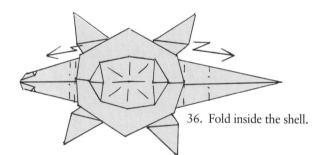

36. Fold inside the shell.

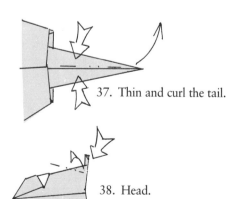

37. Thin and curl the tail.

38. Head.

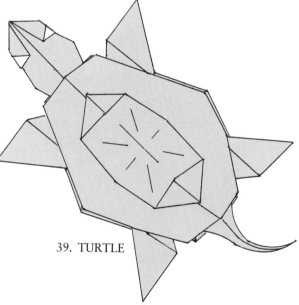

39. TURTLE

FROG

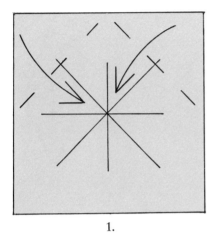

1.

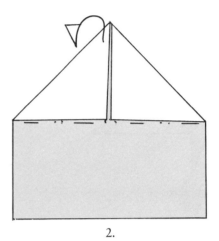

2.

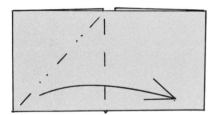

3. Squash-fold.

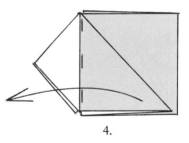

4.

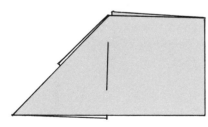

5. Repeat steps 3 & 4 on the right side.

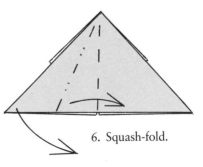

6. Squash-fold.

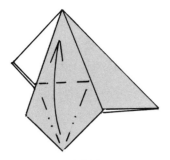

7. Petal-fold.

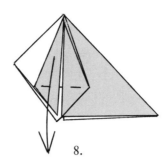

8.

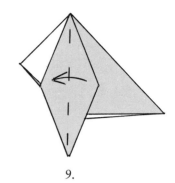

9.

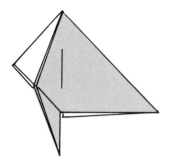

10. Repeat steps 6–9 on the right side.

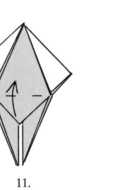

11.

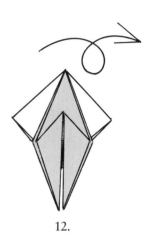

12.

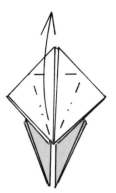

13. Petal-fold.

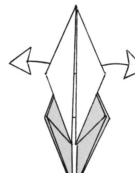

14. Pull out paper from inside.

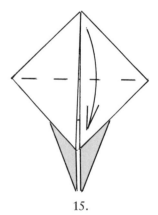

15.

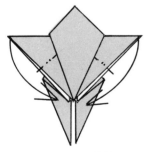

16. Reverse-folds.

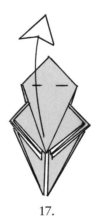

17.

18.

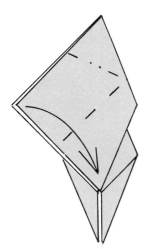

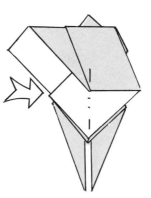

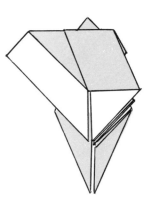

19. Squash-fold.

20. Reverse-fold.

21. Unfold to step 18.

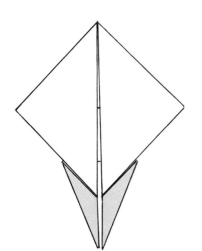

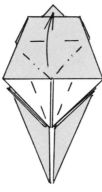

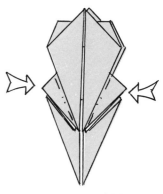

22. Repeat steps 18–21 on the left and, using these new creases, fold them together to form step 23.

23. Petal-fold.

24. Reverse-folds.

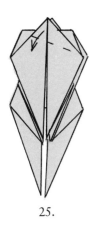

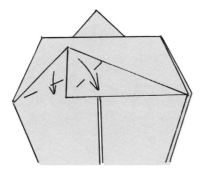

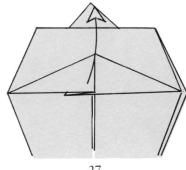

25.

26.

27.

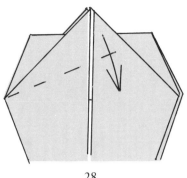

28.

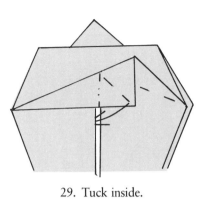

29. Tuck inside.

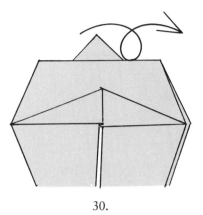

30.

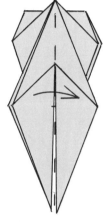

31.

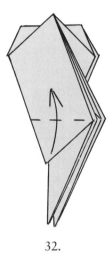

32.

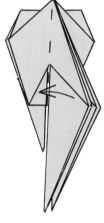

33.

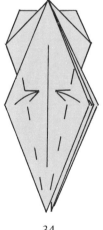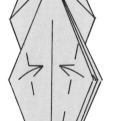

34.

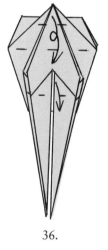

35. Repeat steps 31–35 on the right side.

36.

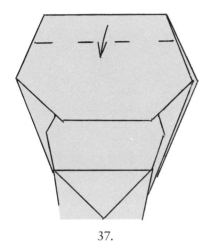

37.

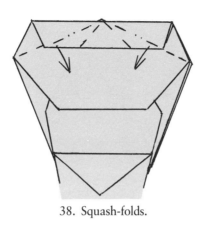

38. Squash-folds.

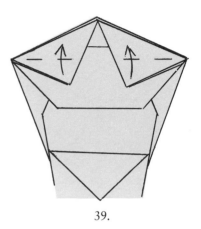

39.

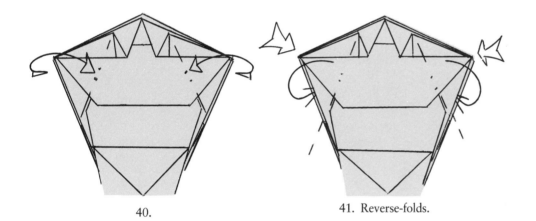

40.

41. Reverse-folds.

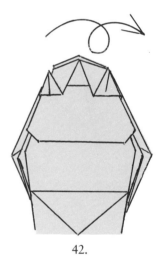

42.

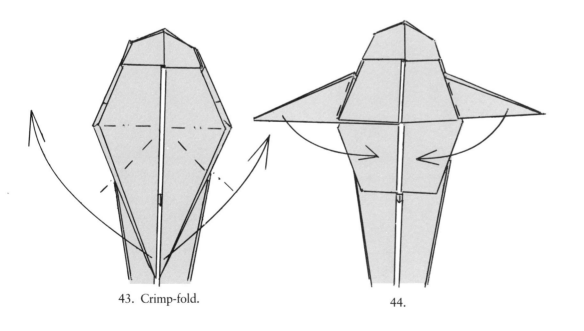

43. Crimp-fold.

44.

45.

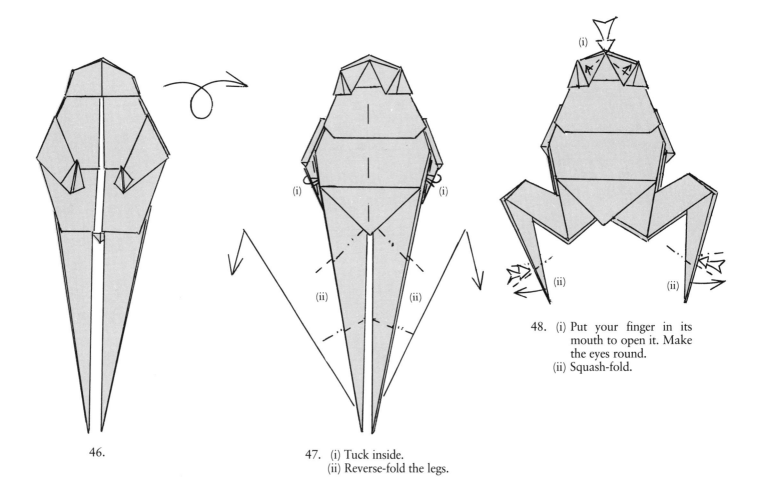

46.

47. (i) Tuck inside.
(ii) Reverse-fold the legs.

48. (i) Put your finger in its
mouth to open it. Make
the eyes round.
(ii) Squash-fold.

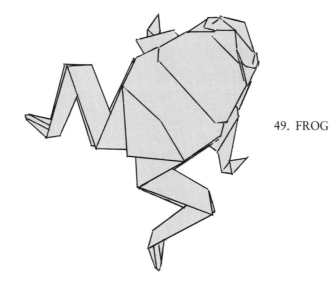

49. FROG

FROG WITH TOES

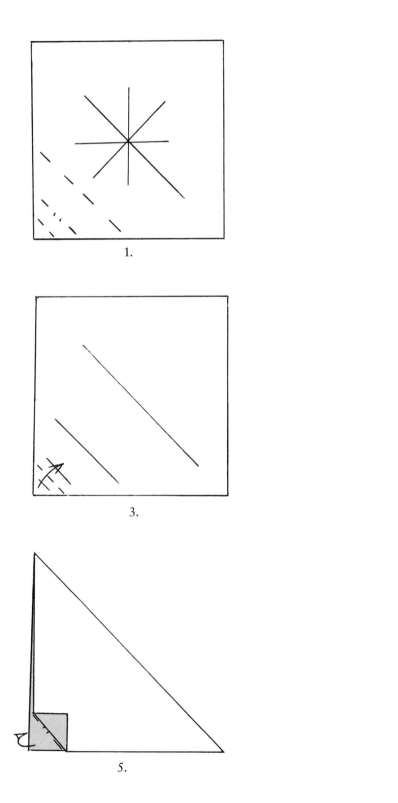

1.

2.

3.

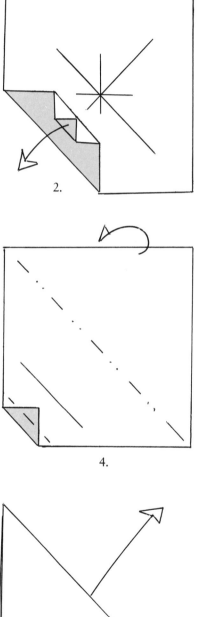

4.

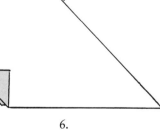

5.

6.

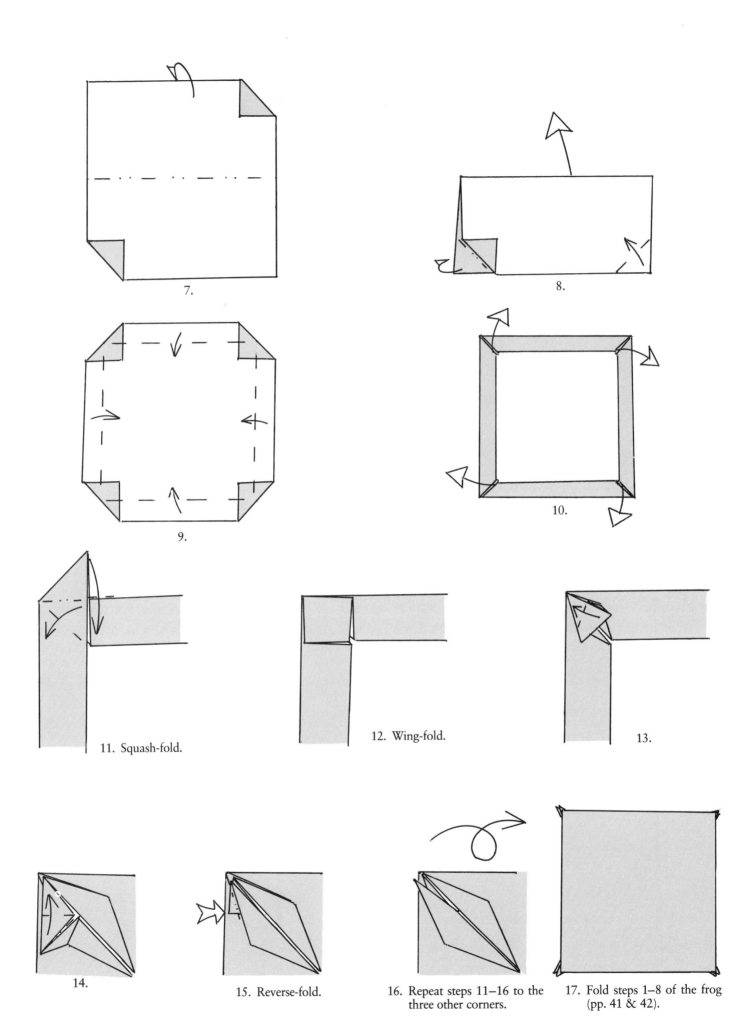

7.

8.

9.

10.

11. Squash-fold.

12. Wing-fold.

13.

14.

15. Reverse-fold.

16. Repeat steps 11–16 to the three other corners.

17. Fold steps 1–8 of the frog (pp. 41 & 42).

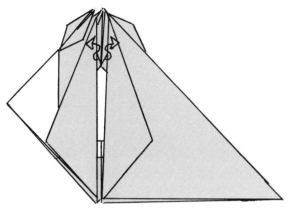

18. Untuck this flap.

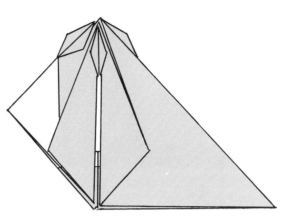

19. Continue with steps 8–44 of the frog.

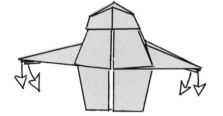

20. Pull out the toes.

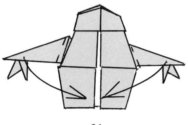

21.

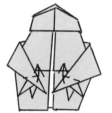

22. Continue with steps 46–48 of the frog.

23a.

23b. Separate the toes.

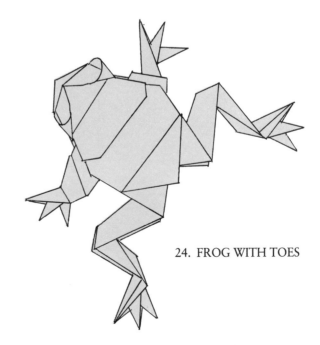

24. FROG WITH TOES

BEAR

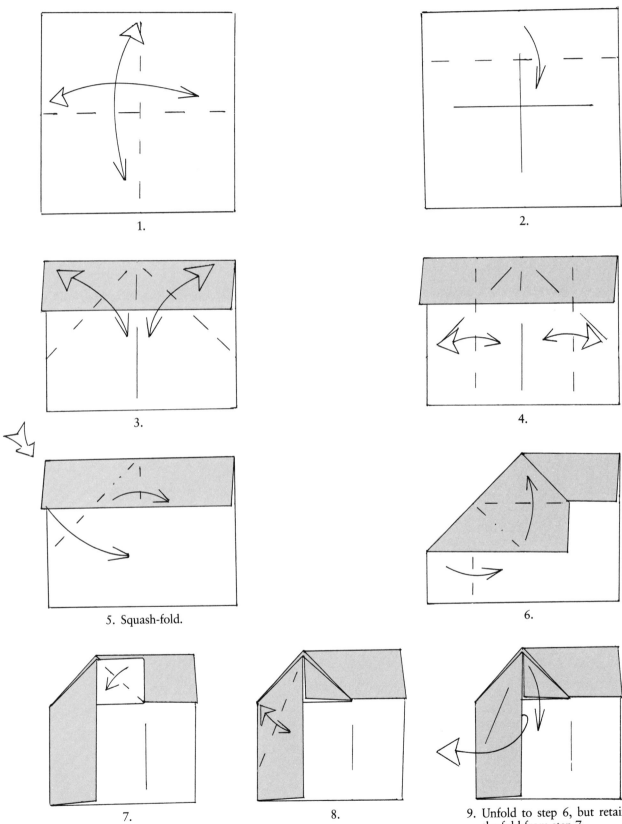

1.

2.

3.

4.

5. Squash-fold.

6.

7.

8.

9. Unfold to step 6, but retain the fold from step 7.

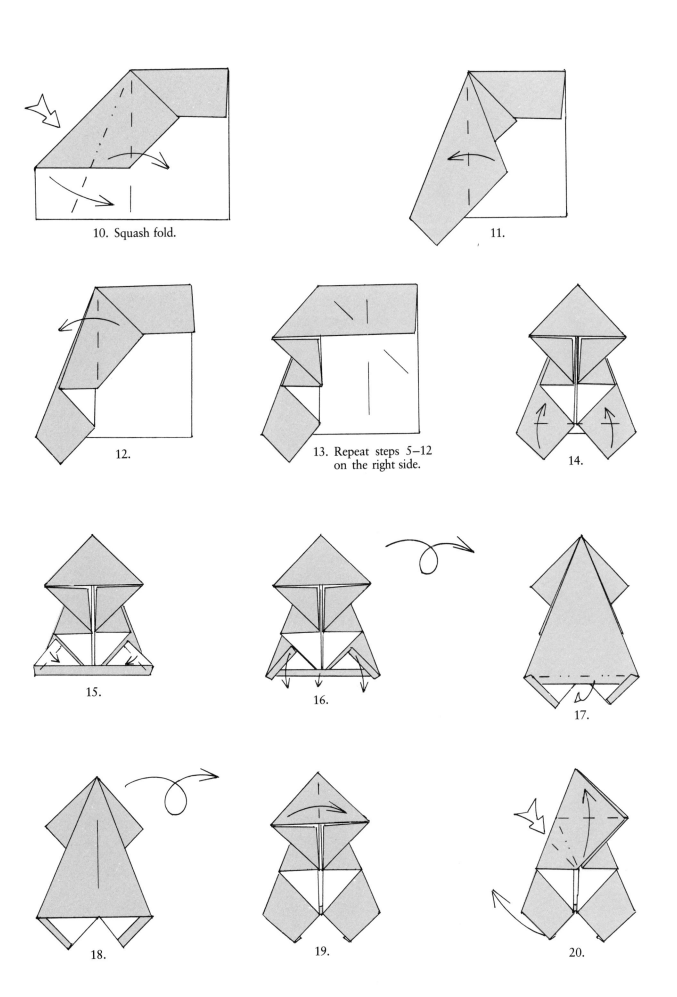

10. Squash fold.

11.

12.

13. Repeat steps 5–12 on the right side.

14.

15.

16.

17.

18.

19.

20.

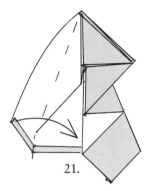

21.

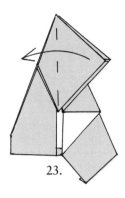

22.

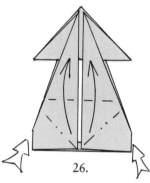

23.

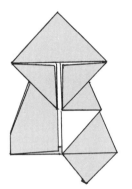

24. Repeat steps 19–23 on the right side.

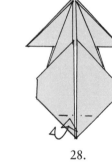

25.

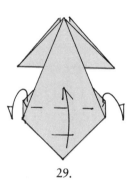

26.

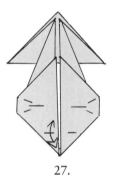

27.

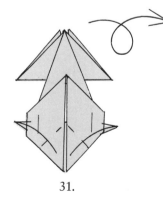

28.

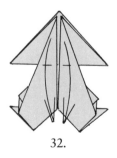

29.

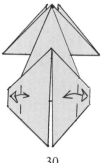

30.

31.

32.

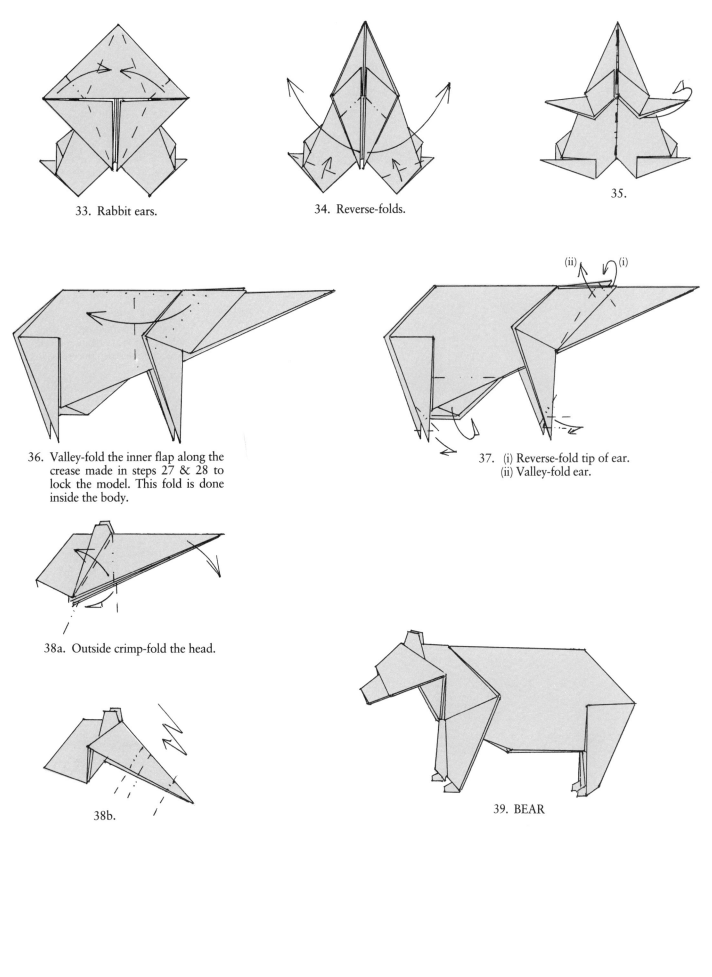

33. Rabbit ears.

34. Reverse-folds.

35.

36. Valley-fold the inner flap along the crease made in steps 27 & 28 to lock the model. This fold is done inside the body.

37. (i) Reverse-fold tip of ear.
(ii) Valley-fold ear.

38a. Outside crimp-fold the head.

38b.

39. BEAR

KANGAROO

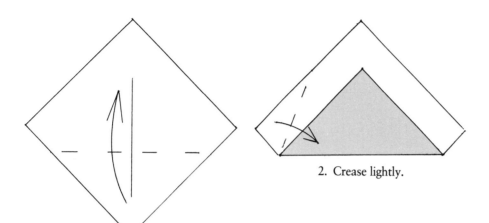

1. Crease lightly.

2. Crease lightly.

3. Check if A & B are on the same horizontal line. If not, adjust the folds from steps 1 & 2, then sharpen the creases.

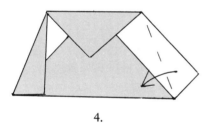

4.

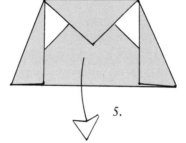

5.

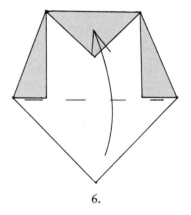

6.

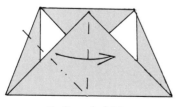

7. Squash-fold.

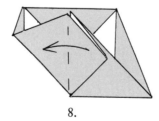

8.

9. Repeat steps 7 & 8 on the right side.

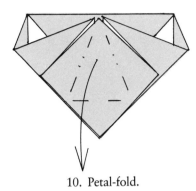

10. Petal-fold.

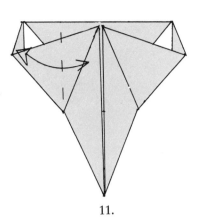

11.

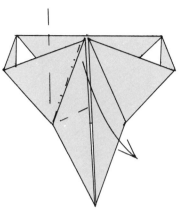

12. Squash-fold.

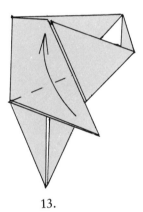

13.

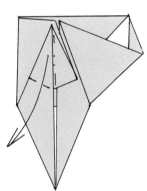

14. Squash-fold. Repeat steps 11–14 on the right side.

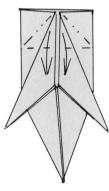

15. Squash-folds.

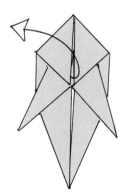

16. Pull out the inner flap (that was folded down in step 3).

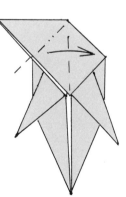

17. Squash-fold.

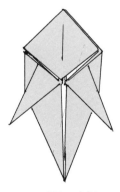

18. Wing-fold.

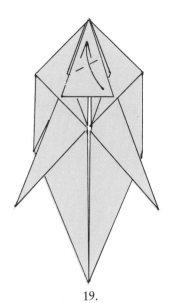

19.

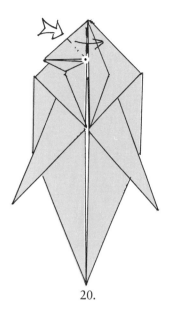

20.

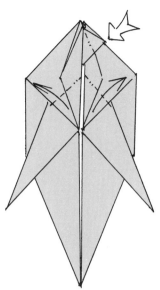

21. Reverse-folds.

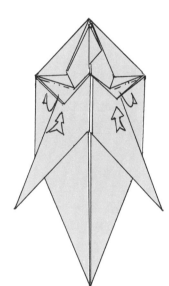

22. Reverse-folds.

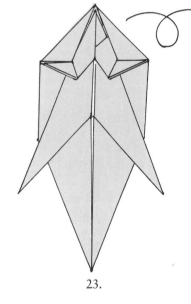

23.

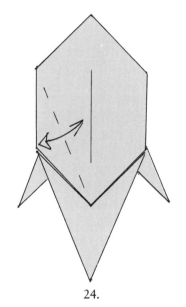

24.

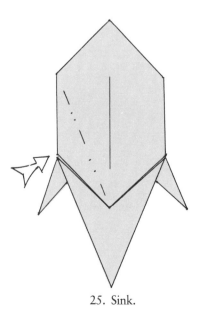

25. Sink.

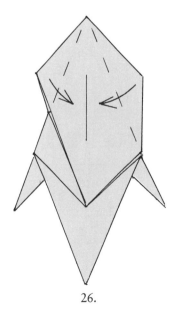

26.

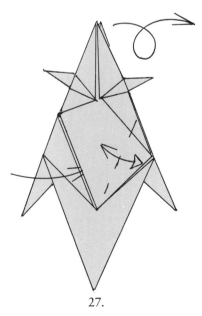

27.

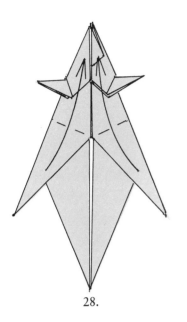

28.

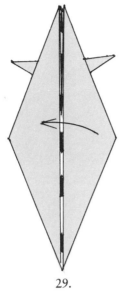

29.

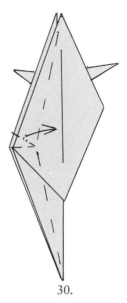

30.

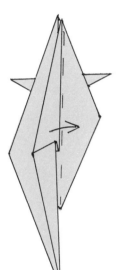

31. Repeat steps 29–31 on the left side.

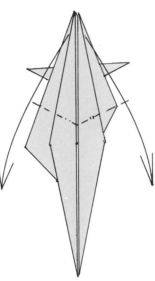

32. Reverse-folds.

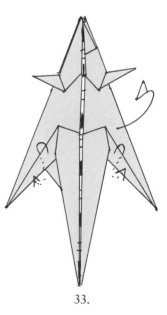

33.

34. Outside reverse-fold.

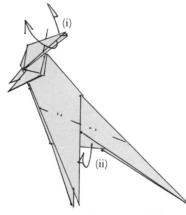

35. (i) Outside reverse-fold.
(ii) Tuck inside the pocket.

36. Outside crimp-fold.

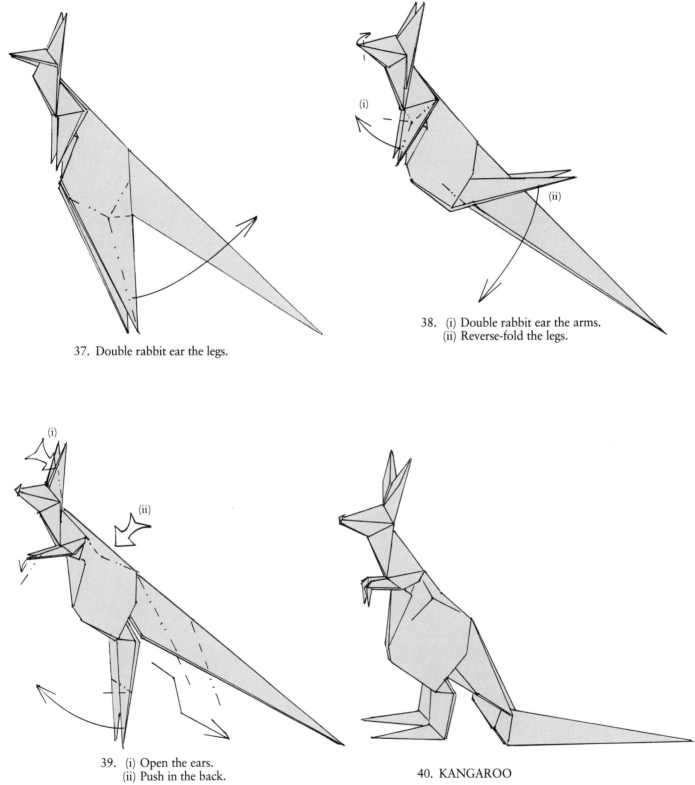

37. Double rabbit ear the legs.

38. (i) Double rabbit ear the arms.
    (ii) Reverse-fold the legs.

39. (i) Open the ears.
    (ii) Push in the back.

40. KANGAROO

GIRAFFE

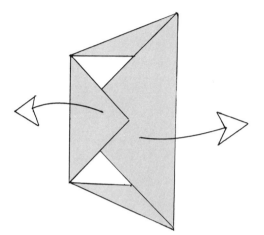

1. Begin with step 5 of the kangaroo (p. 54).

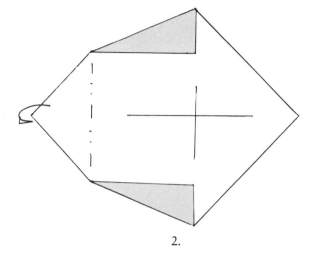

2.

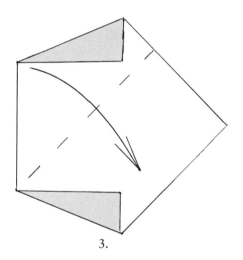

3.

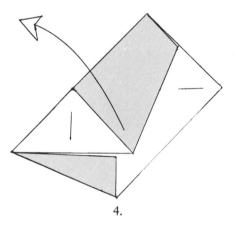

4.

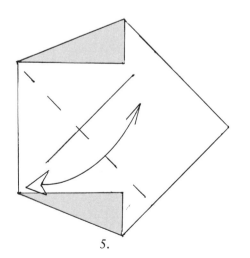

5.

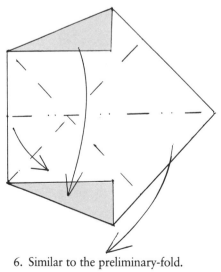

6. Similar to the preliminary-fold.

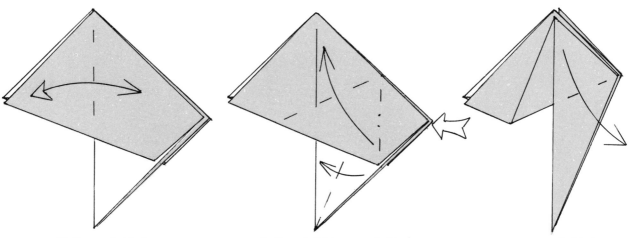

7. Repeat behind.

8. Squash-fold; repeat behind.

9. Repeat behind.

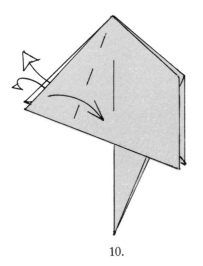

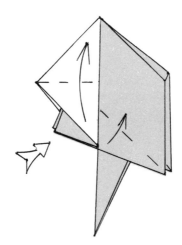

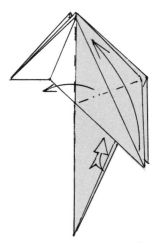

10.

11. Squash-fold; repeat behind.

12. Squash-fold; repeat behind.

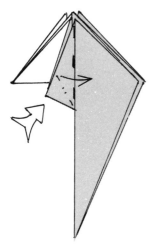

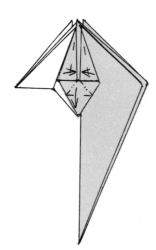

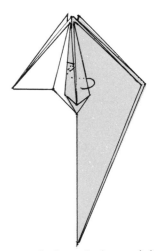

13. Squash-fold; repeat behind.

14. Petal-fold; repeat behind.

15. Tuck the right layer of the petal-fold under one layer; repeat behind.

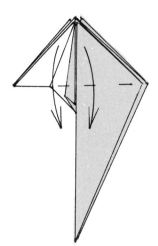

16. Repeat behind.

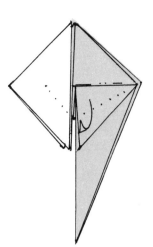

17. Mountain-fold the inner flap up and into the body; repeat behind.

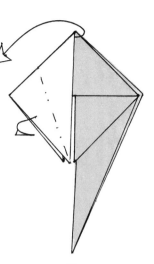

18.

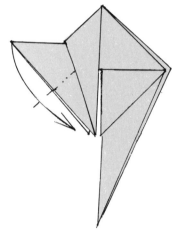

19. Reverse-fold.

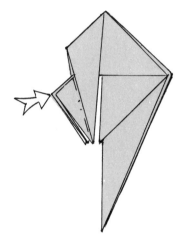

20. Reverse-fold. Repeat behind.

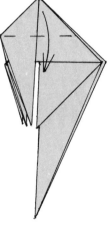

21.

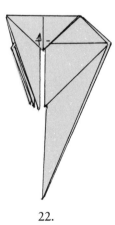

22.

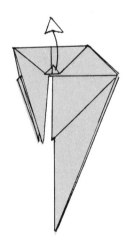

23. Unfold to step 21.

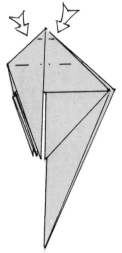

24. Sink triangularly.

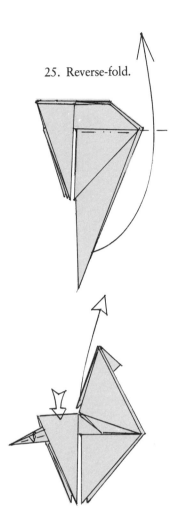

25. Reverse-fold.

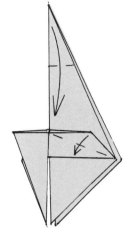

26. Repeat behind.

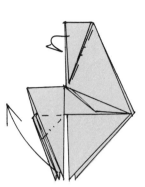

27. Crimp-fold the tail.

28. Reverse-fold to thin the tail;
    repeat behind.

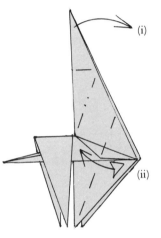

29. (i) Reverse-fold.
    (ii) Repeat behind.

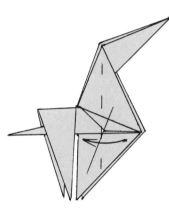

30. Repeat behind.

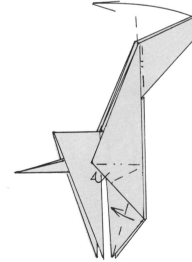

31. Reverse-fold; repeat behind.

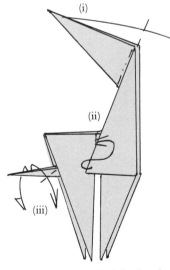

32. (i) Reverse-fold the head.
    (ii) Tuck. Repeat behind.
    (iii) Outside reverse-fold the tail.

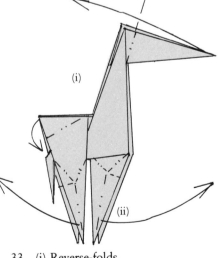

33. (i) Reverse-folds.
    (ii) Double rabbit ear the legs;
    repeat behind.

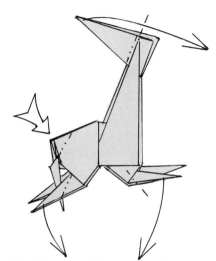

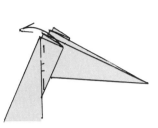

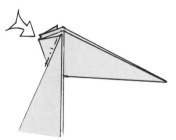

34. All reverse-folds; repeat behind.

35a. Head. Reverse-fold; repeat behind.

35b. Reverse-fold; repeat behind.

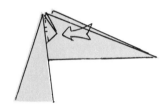

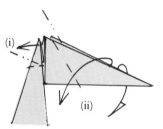

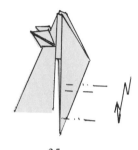

35c. Reverse-fold; repeat behind.

35d. (i) Squash-fold; repeat behind.
(ii) Outside reverse-fold the head. Note that it does not come to a point at the horns.

35e.

35f. Crimp-fold.

36. GIRAFFE

FOX

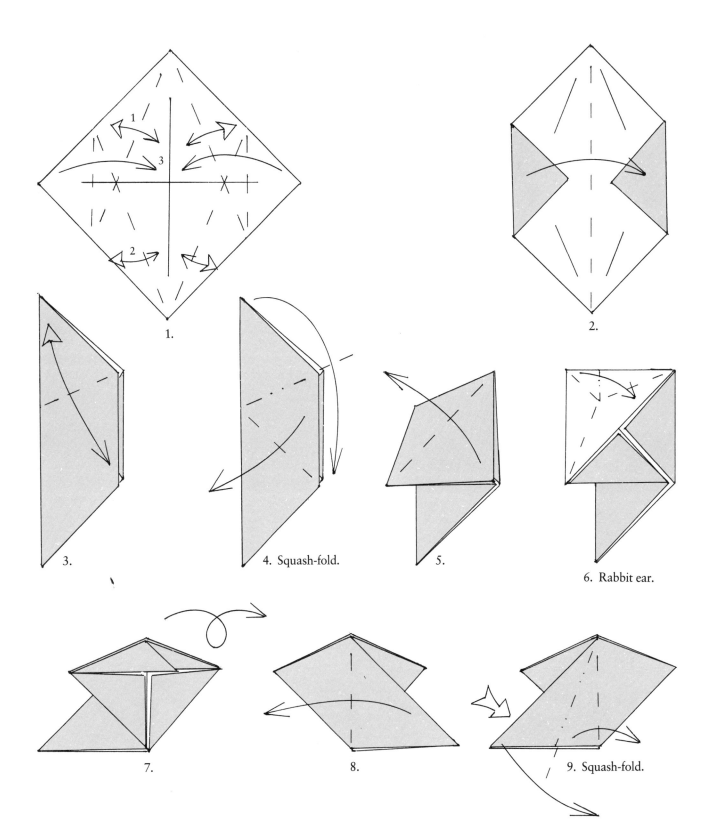

1.

2.

3.

4. Squash-fold.

5.

6. Rabbit ear.

7.

8.

9. Squash-fold.

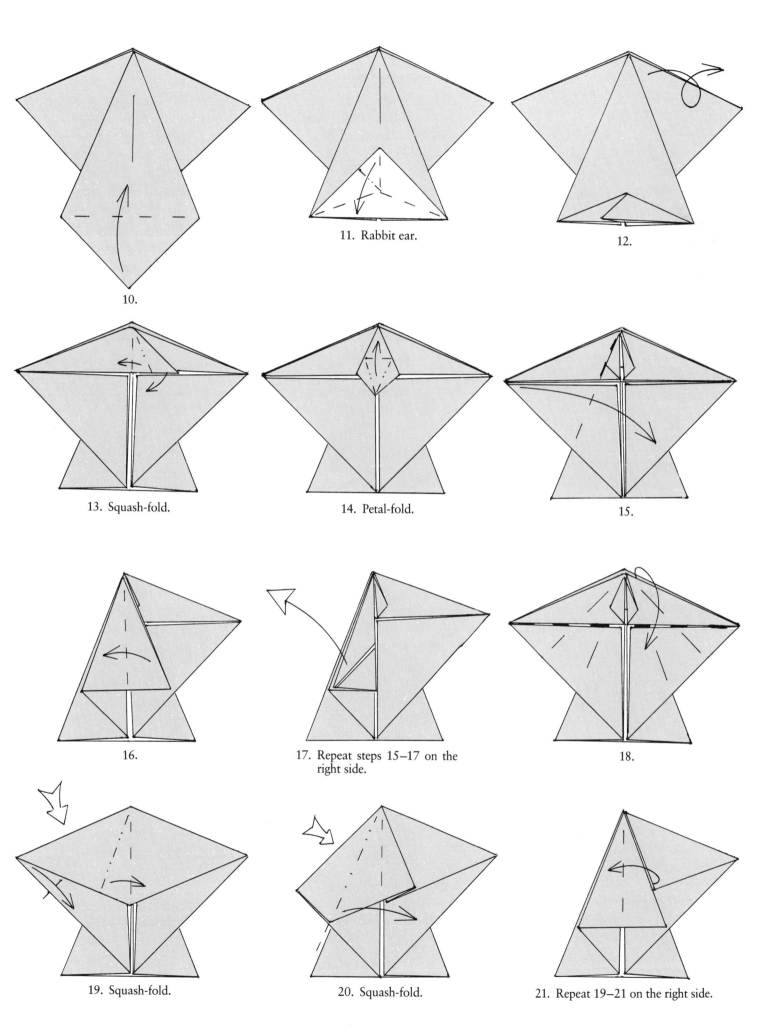

10.

11. Rabbit ear.

12.

13. Squash-fold.

14. Petal-fold.

15.

16.

17. Repeat steps 15–17 on the right side.

18.

19. Squash-fold.

20. Squash-fold.

21. Repeat 19–21 on the right side.

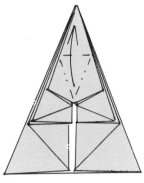

22. Unlock to fold up.

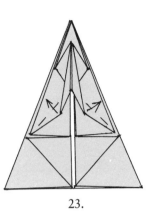

23.

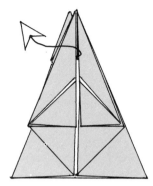

24. Pull out the flap.

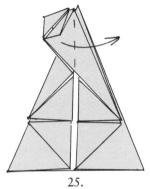

25.

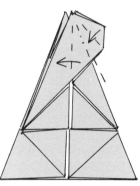

26. Squash-fold.

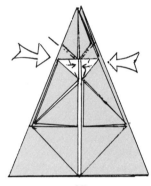

27.

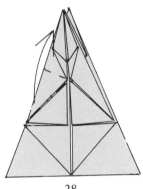

28.

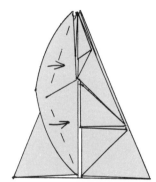

29. Repeat steps 28 & 29 on the right side.

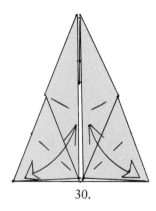

30.

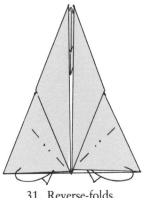

31. Reverse-folds.

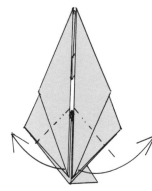

32. Reverse-folds.

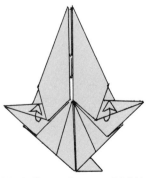

33. Pull out a layer and fold it on top. This is similar to an outside reverse-fold.

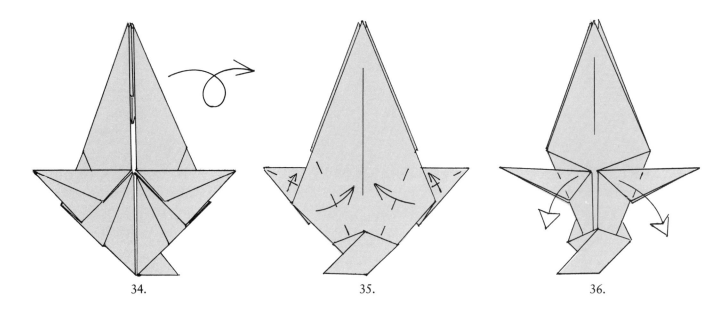

34.

35.

36.

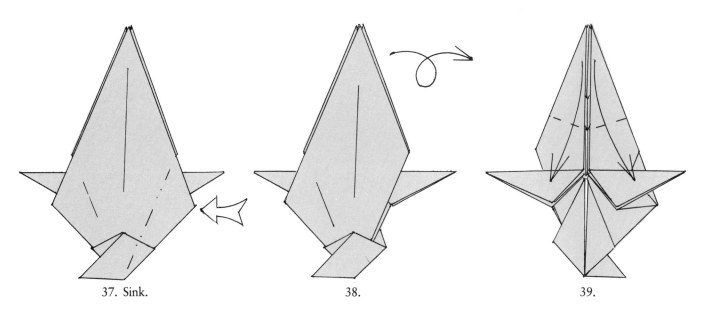

37. Sink.

38.

39.

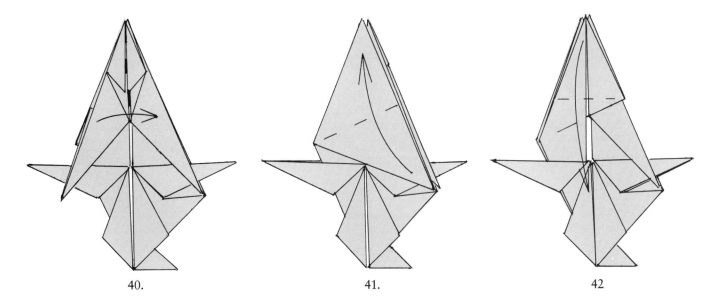

40.

41.

42

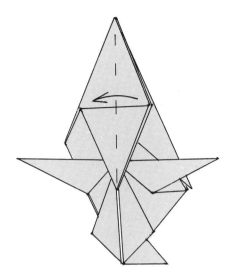

43. Repeat steps 40–43 on the right side.

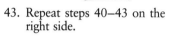

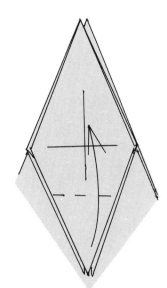

44.

45. Top of the model enlarged.

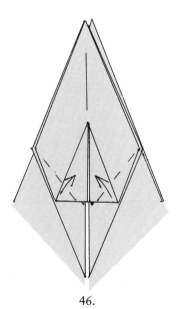

46.

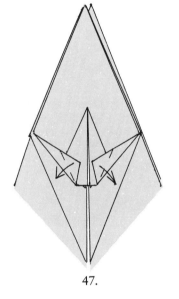

47.

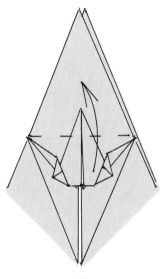

48.

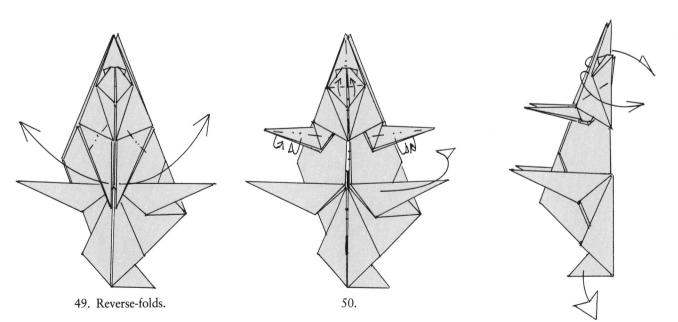

49. Reverse-folds.

50.

51. Pull the tail out.

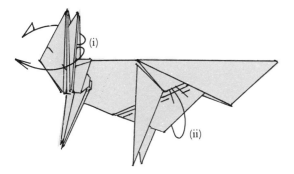

52. (i) Outside reverse-fold the head.
    (ii) Fold inside the pocket to lock
    the animal.

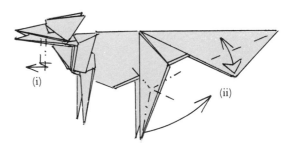

53. (i) Crimp-fold the mouth.
    (ii) Double rabbit ear the legs.

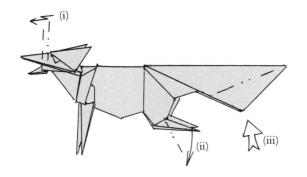

54. (i) Crimp-fold.
    (ii) Reverse-fold the legs.
    (iii) Sink.

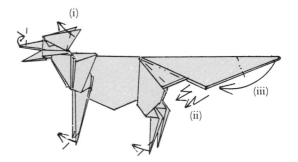

55. (i) Outside reverse-fold to form
    the nose.
    (ii) Crimp the tail down.
    (iii) Reverse-fold the tip of the tail.

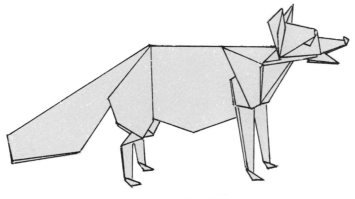

56. FOX

ELEPHANT

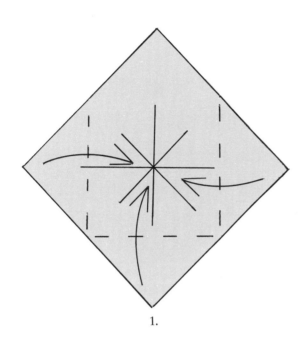

1.

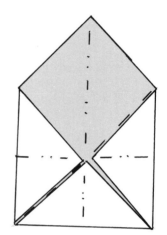

2. Similar to the preliminary-fold.

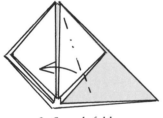

3. Squash-fold.

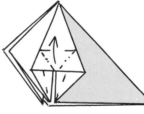

4. Petal-fold.

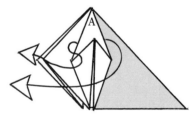

5. Unfold the original corner out.

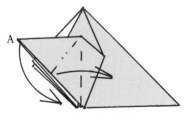

6. Squash-fold.

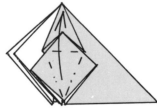

7. Petal-fold.

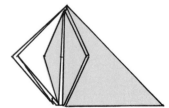

8. Repeat steps 3–7 behind.

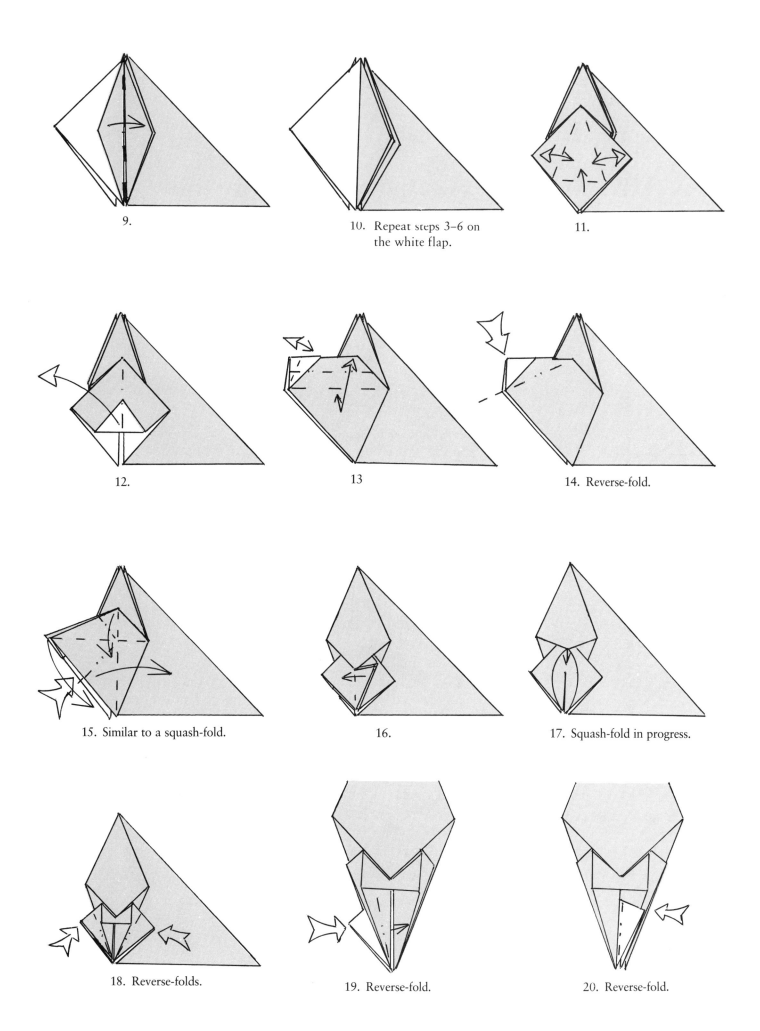

9.

10. Repeat steps 3–6 on the white flap.

11.

12.

13

14. Reverse-fold.

15. Similar to a squash-fold.

16.

17. Squash-fold in progress.

18. Reverse-folds.

19. Reverse-fold.

20. Reverse-fold.

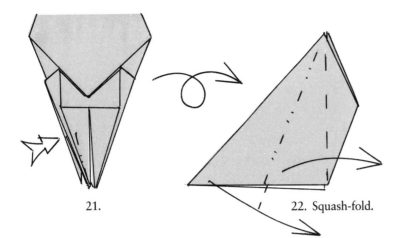

21.

22. Squash-fold.

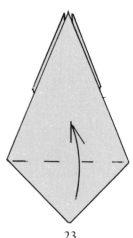

23.

24.

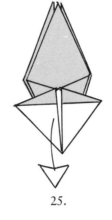

25.

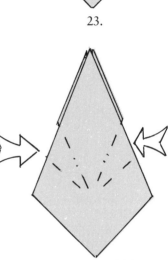

26. Crimp-folds.

27.

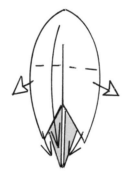

28. Flatten.

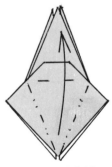

29. Petal-fold.

30.

31.

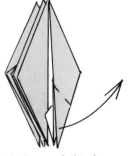

32. Repeat behind.

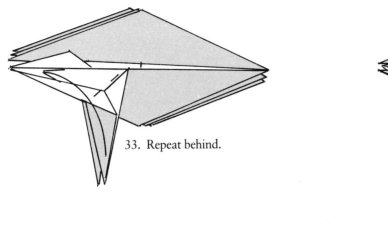

33. Repeat behind.

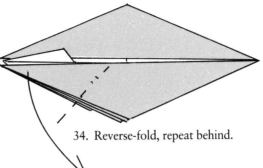

34. Reverse-fold, repeat behind.

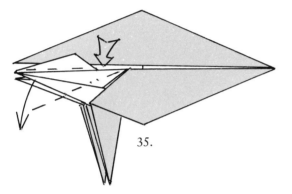

35.

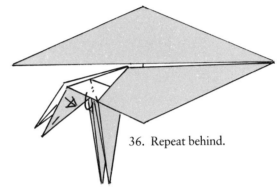

36. Repeat behind.

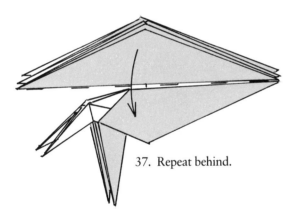

37. Repeat behind.

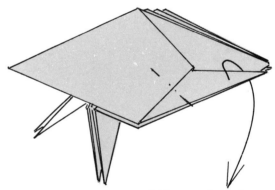

38. Simple mountain-fold; repeat behind.

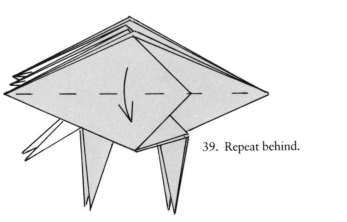

39. Repeat behind.

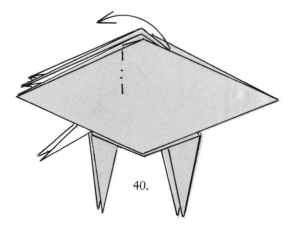

40.

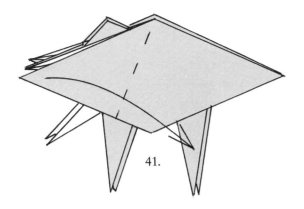

41.

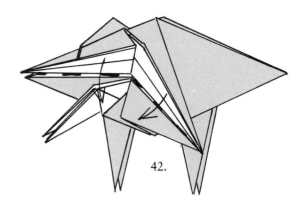

42.

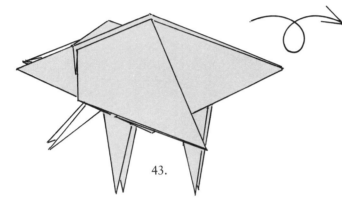

43.

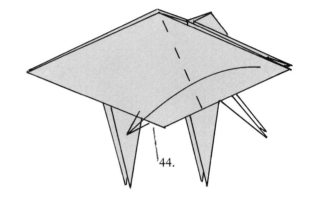

44.

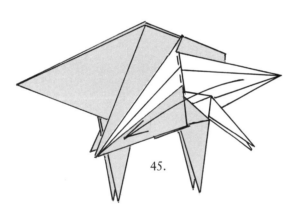

45.

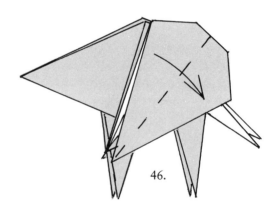

46.

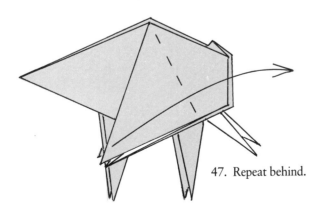

47. Repeat behind.

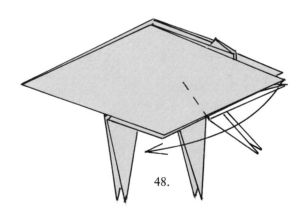

48.

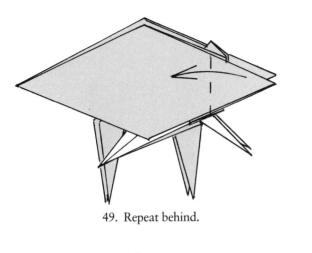

49. Repeat behind.

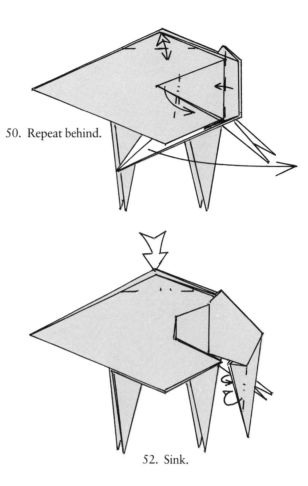

50. Repeat behind.

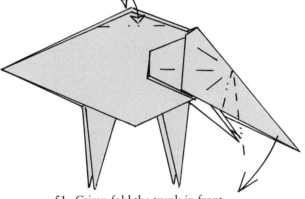

51. Crimp-fold the trunk in front of the tusks.

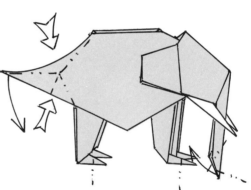

52. Sink.

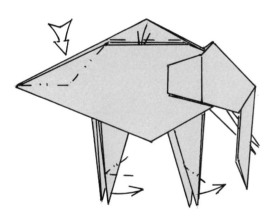

53. Put the trunk between the tusks.

54. The folds for the tail are similar to the double rabbit ear.

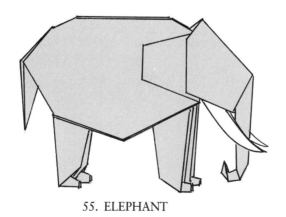

55. ELEPHANT

ANTELOPE

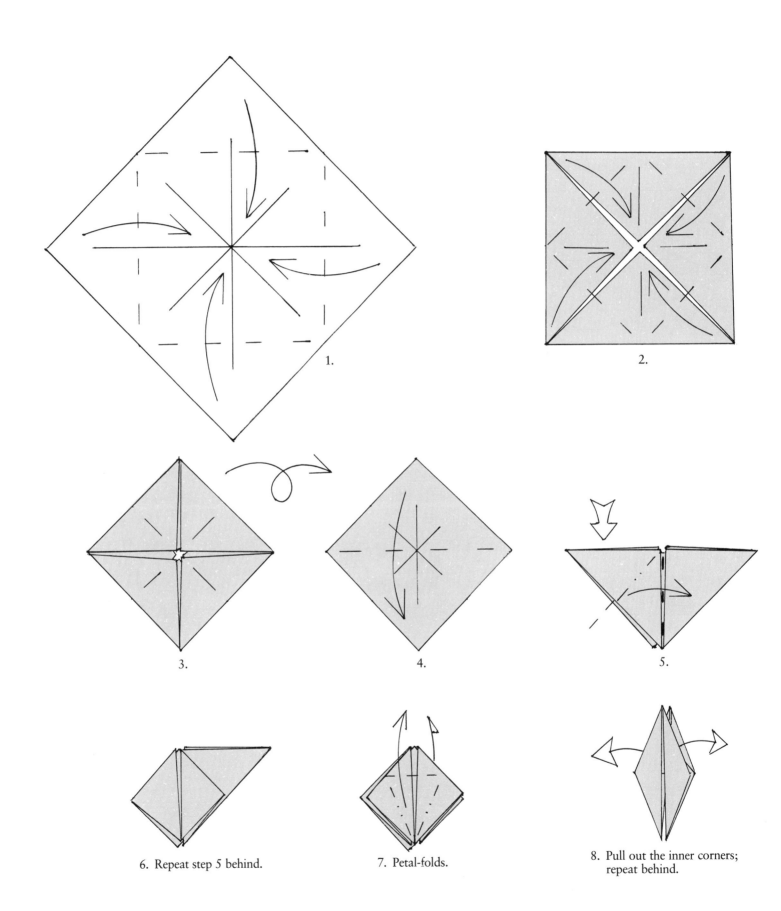

1.

2.

3.

4.

5.

6. Repeat step 5 behind.

7. Petal-folds.

8. Pull out the inner corners; repeat behind.

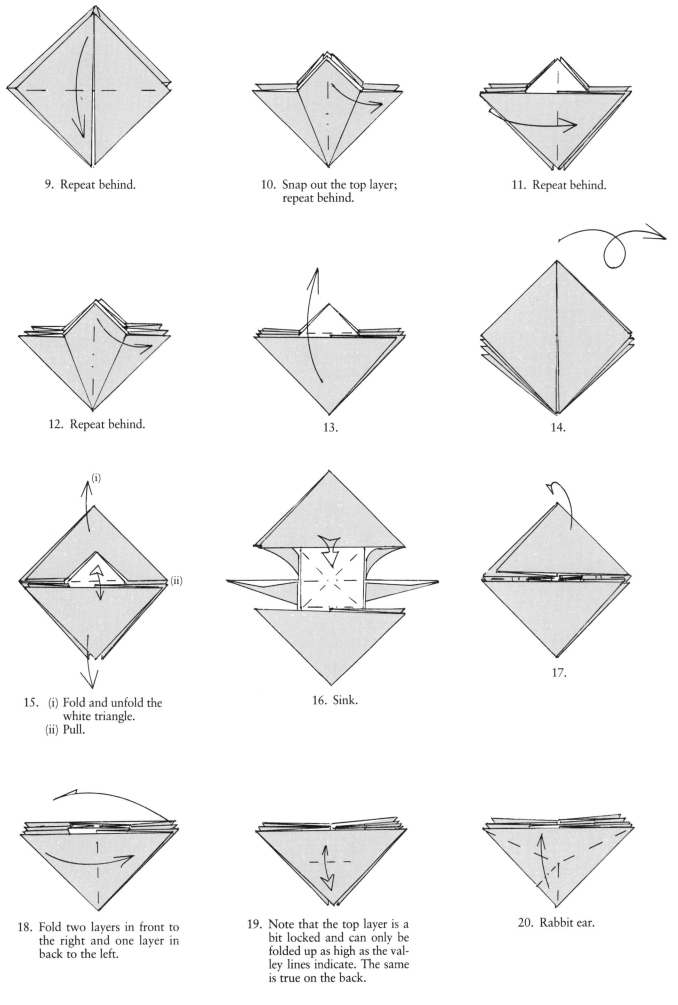

9. Repeat behind.

10. Snap out the top layer; repeat behind.

11. Repeat behind.

12. Repeat behind.

13.

14.

15. (i) Fold and unfold the white triangle.
    (ii) Pull.

16. Sink.

17.

18. Fold two layers in front to the right and one layer in back to the left.

19. Note that the top layer is a bit locked and can only be folded up as high as the valley lines indicate. The same is true on the back.

20. Rabbit ear.

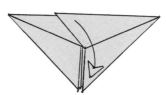

21. Unfold the rabbit ear.

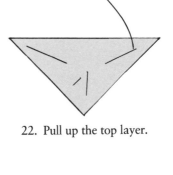

22. Pull up the top layer.

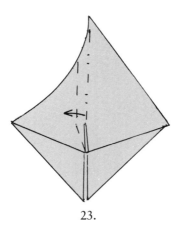

23.

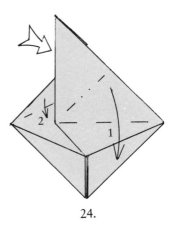

24.

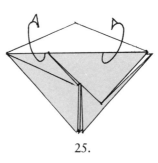

25.

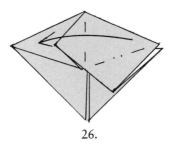

26.

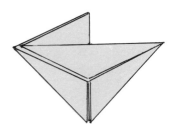

27. Repeat steps 20–26 behind.

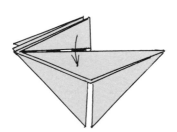

28. Repeat behind.

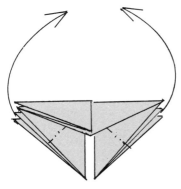

29. Pull out the middle flaps.

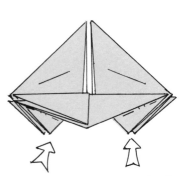

30. Reverse-folds; repeat behind.

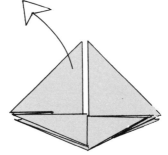

31. Pull out carefully.

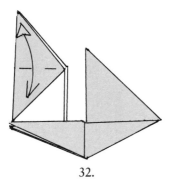

32.

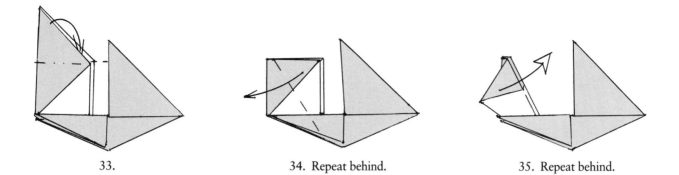

33.   34. Repeat behind.   35. Repeat behind.

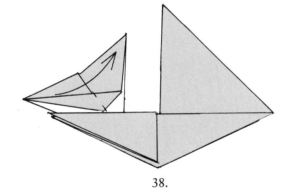

36. Reverse-fold.

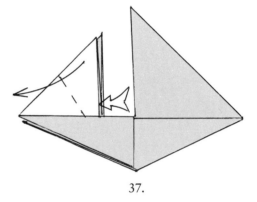

37.

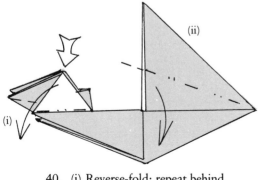

38.

39. Repeat steps 37–39 behind.

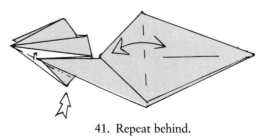

40. (i) Reverse-fold; repeat behind.
    (ii) Squash-fold.

41. Repeat behind.

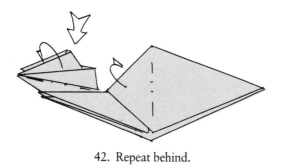

42. Repeat behind.

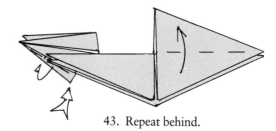

43. Repeat behind.

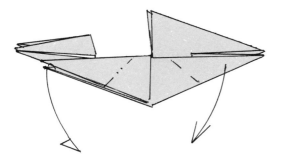

44. Mountain-fold the front legs; repeat behind.

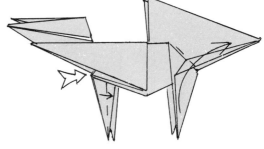

45. Repeat behind.

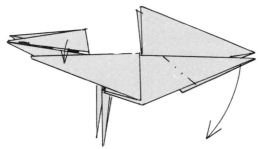

46. Reverse-fold (two layers above, one below); repeat behind.

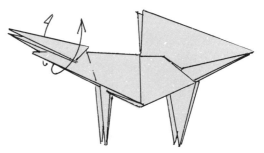

47. Outside reverse-fold.

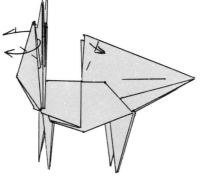

48. Outside reverse-fold to form the head.

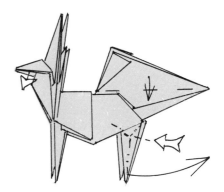

49. Pull out paper from inside the head. Double rabbit ear the hind legs; repeat behind.

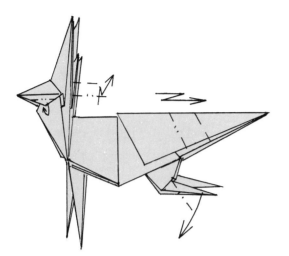

50. Crimp the ears and tail; repeat behind.

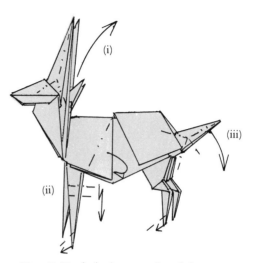

51. (i) Pinch the horns and curl them; repeat behind.
(ii) Crimp the front legs.
(iii) Double rabbit ear the tail.

ANTELOPE

SPIDER

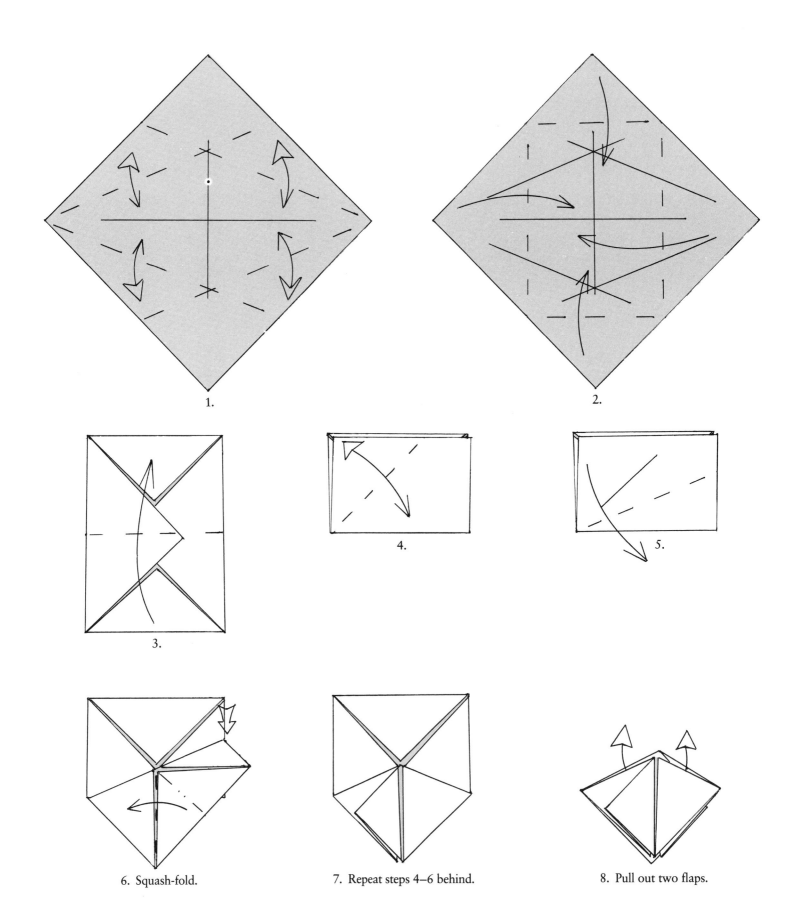

1.

2.

3.

4.

5.

6. Squash-fold.

7. Repeat steps 4–6 behind.

8. Pull out two flaps.

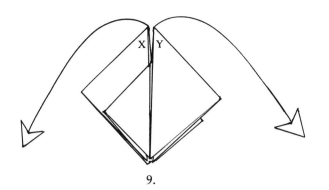

9.

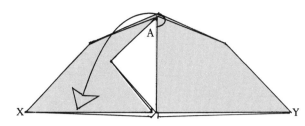

10. (Do not repeat behind)

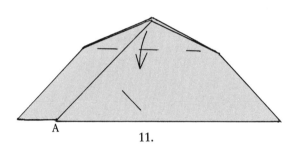

11.

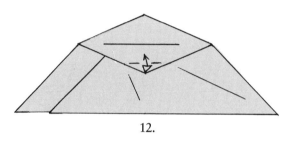

12.

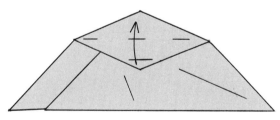

13.

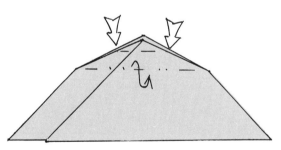

14. Sink triangularly.

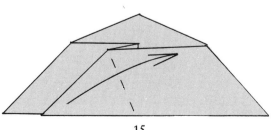

15.

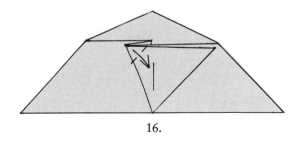

16.

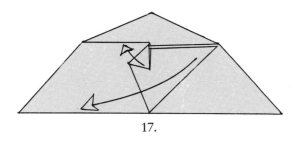

17.

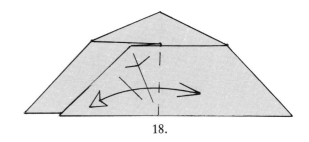

18.

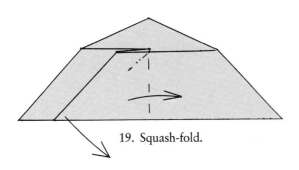

19. Squash-fold.

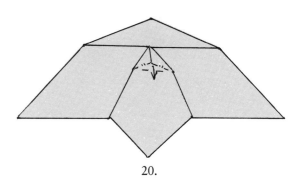

20.

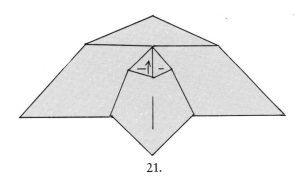

21.

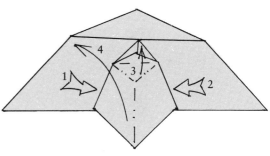

22. Fold along existing creases.

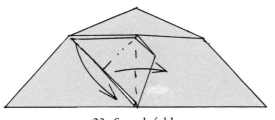

23. Squash-fold.

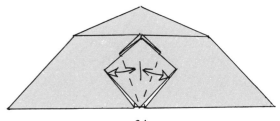

24.

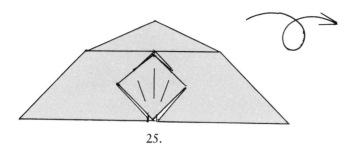

25.

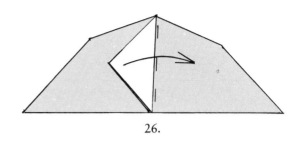

26.

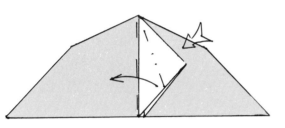

27. Squash-fold.

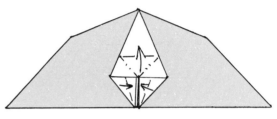

28. Petal-fold.

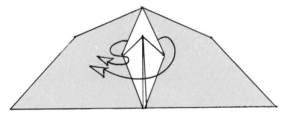

29. Unfold the white layer.

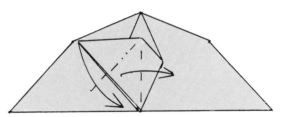

30. Squash-fold.

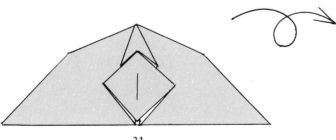

31.

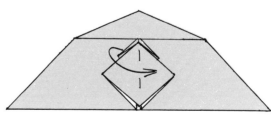

32. Repeat behind.

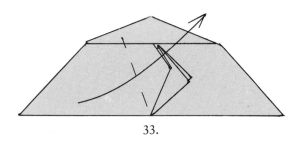

33.

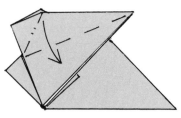

34. Squash-fold.

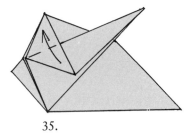

35.

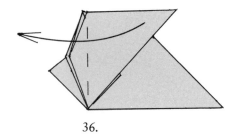

36.

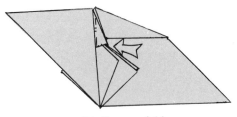

37. Reverse-fold.

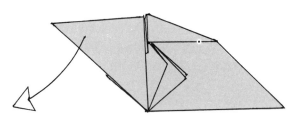

38. Unfold to step 33.

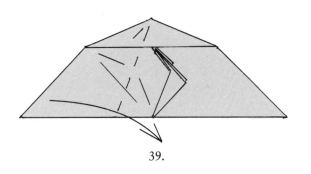

39.

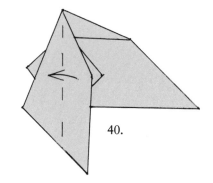

40.

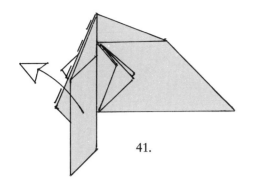

41.

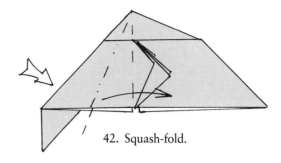

42. Squash-fold.

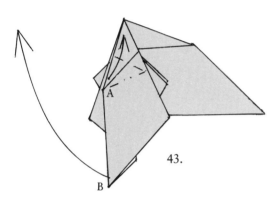

43.

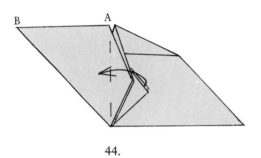

44.

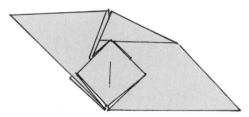

45. Repeat steps 32–44 on the right side.

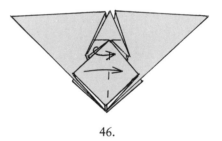

46.

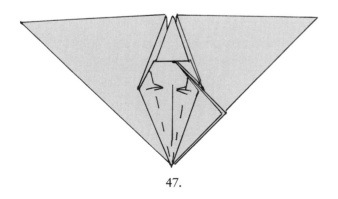

47.

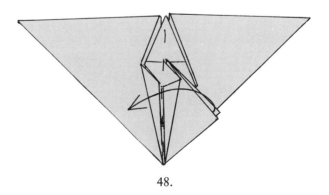

48.

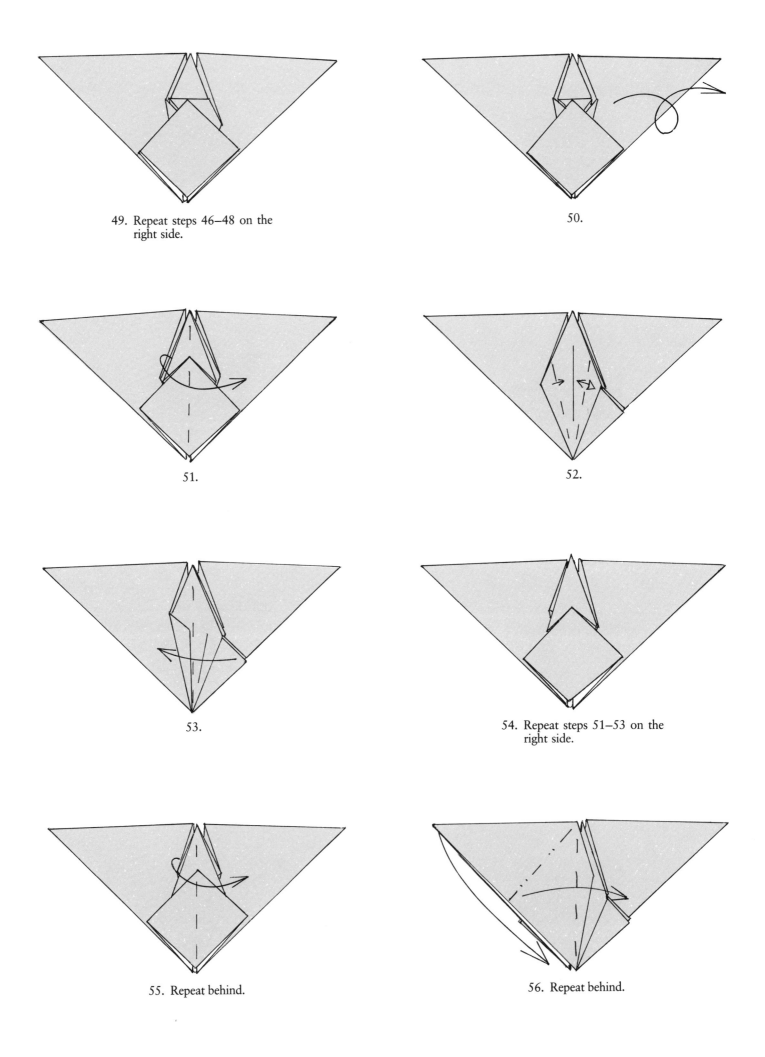

49. Repeat steps 46–48 on the right side.

50.

51.

52.

53.

54. Repeat steps 51–53 on the right side.

55. Repeat behind.

56. Repeat behind.

57. Squash-fold.

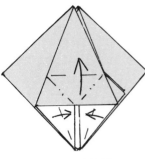

58. Petal-fold.

59.

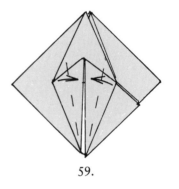

60.

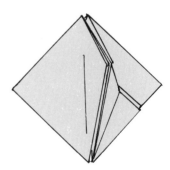

61. Repeat steps 57–60 on the left and behind.

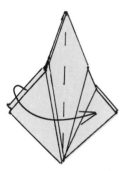

62. Repeat behind.

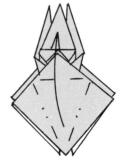

63. Petal-fold.

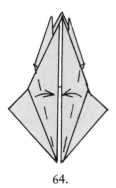

64.

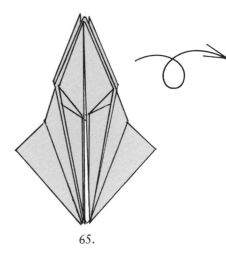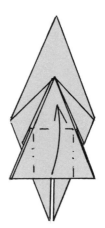

65.   66. Wing-fold.   67. Petal-fold.

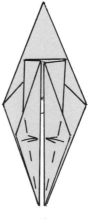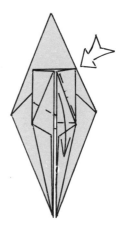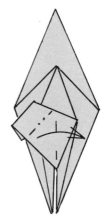

68.   69. Squash-fold.   70. Squash-fold.

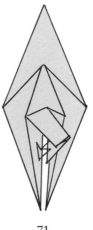

71.   72.   73. Squash-fold.

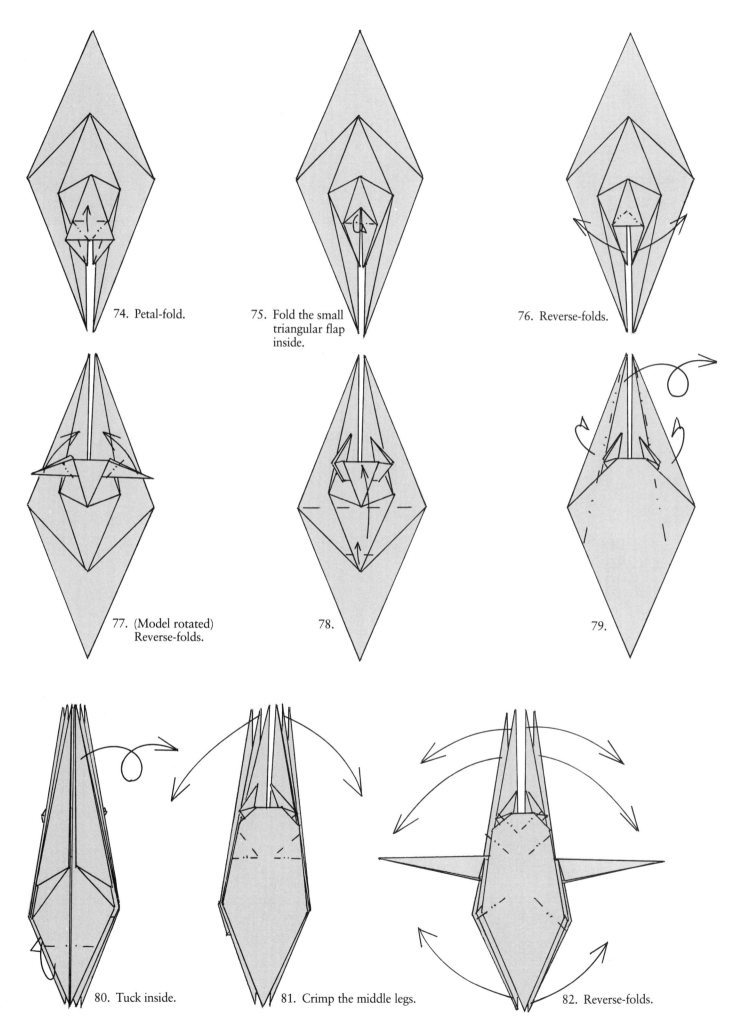

74. Petal-fold.

75. Fold the small triangular flap inside.

76. Reverse-folds.

77. (Model rotated) Reverse-folds.

78.

79.

80. Tuck inside.

81. Crimp the middle legs.

82. Reverse-folds.

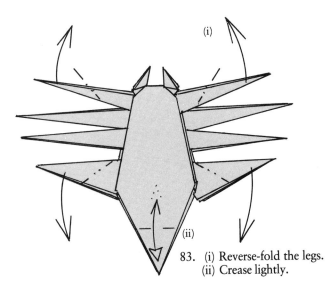

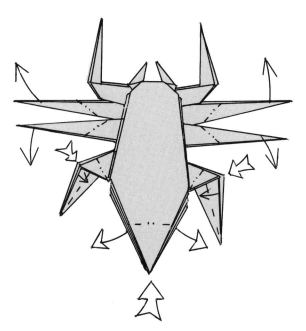

83. (i) Reverse-fold the legs.
    (ii) Crease lightly.

84. Fold a good, even octagon.

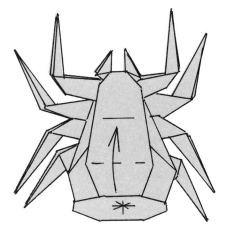

85.

86. SPIDER

CRAB

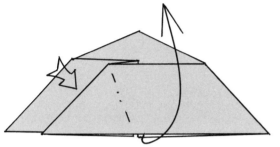

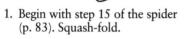

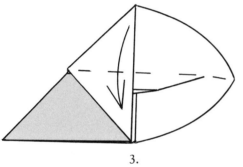

1. Begin with step 15 of the spider (p. 83). Squash-fold.

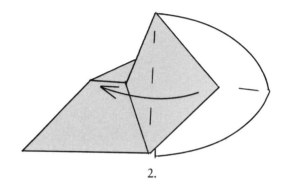

2.

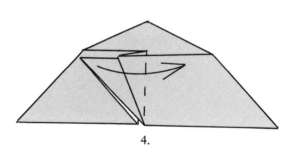

3.

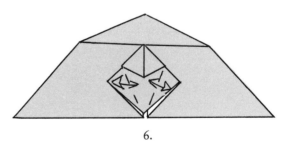

4.

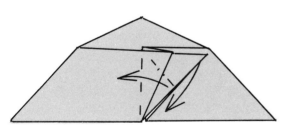

5. Squash-fold.

6.

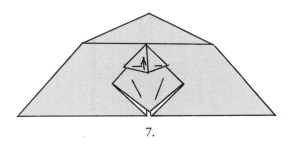

7.

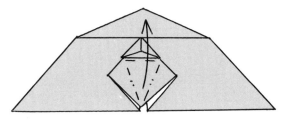

8. Petal-fold.

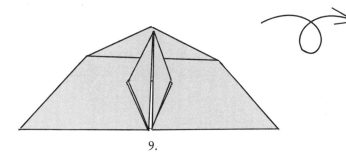

9.

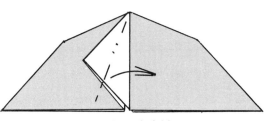

10. Squash-fold.

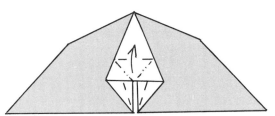

11. Petal-fold.

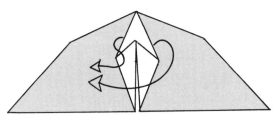

12. Unfold the original corner.

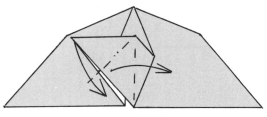

13. Squash-fold.

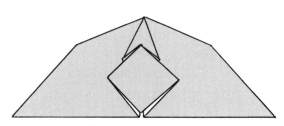

14. Fold half of the brontosaurus base.

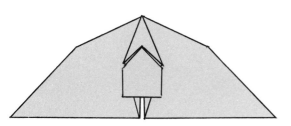

15. Fold the small triangle underneath.

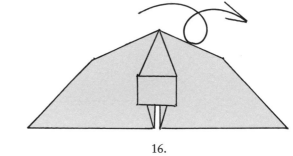

16.

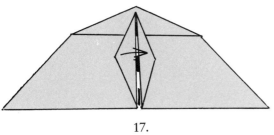

17.

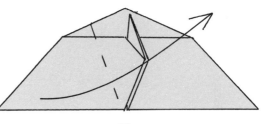

18.

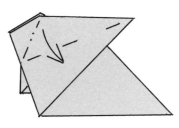

19. Squash-fold.

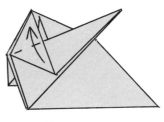

20.

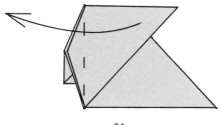

21.

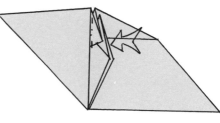

22. Reverse-fold.

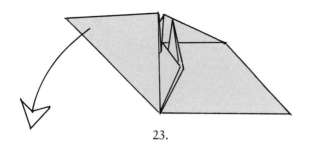

23.

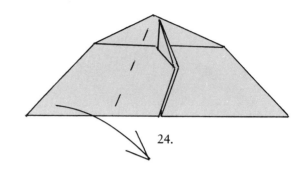

24.

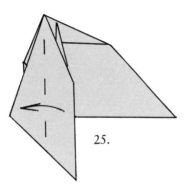

25.

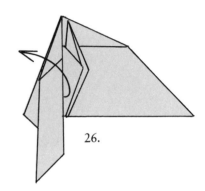

26.

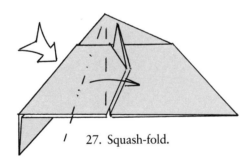

27. Squash-fold.

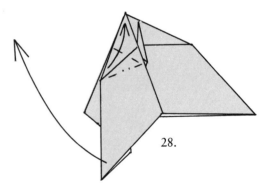

28.

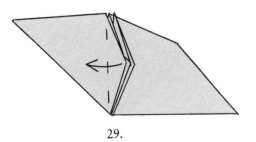

29.

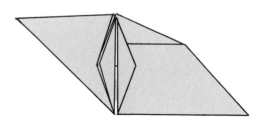

30. Repeat steps 18–29 on the right side.

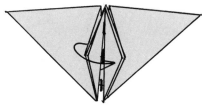

31. Repeat behind.

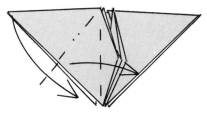

32. Squash-fold; repeat behind.

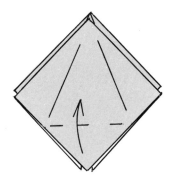

33. Repeat behind.

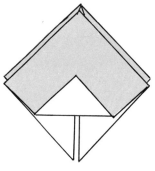

34. Wing-fold.

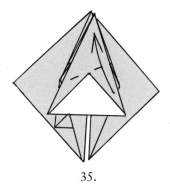

35.

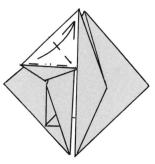

36. Squash-fold.

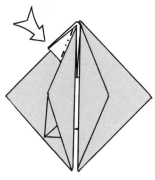

37. Reverse-fold.

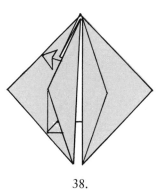

38.

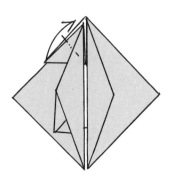

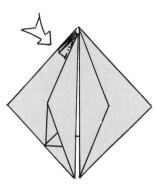

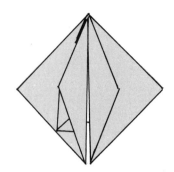

39. Reverse-fold.

40. Reverse-folds.

41. Repeat steps 34–40 behind.

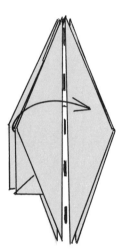

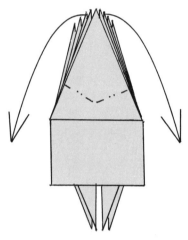

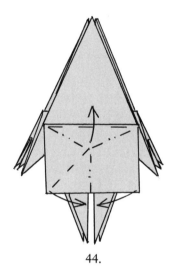

42. Repeat behind.

43. Reverse-fold three of the four flaps together on each side.

44.

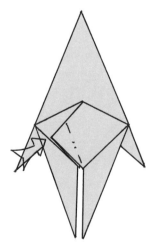

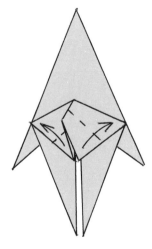

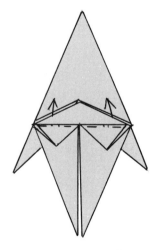

45. Reverse-fold.

46.

47. Reverse-folds.

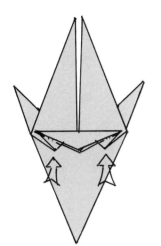

48. (Model rotated) Reverse-folds.

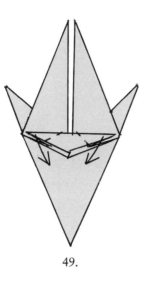

49.

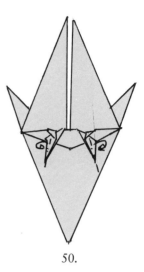

50.

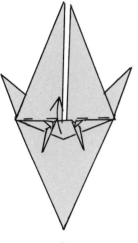

51.

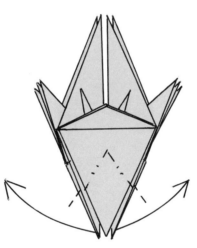

52. Reverse-folds.

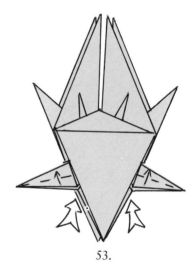

53.

54. Mountain-fold all the layers together.

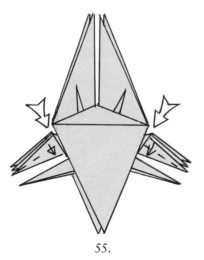

55.

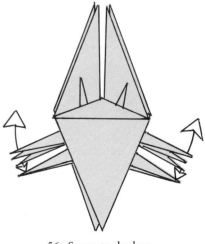

56. Separate the legs.

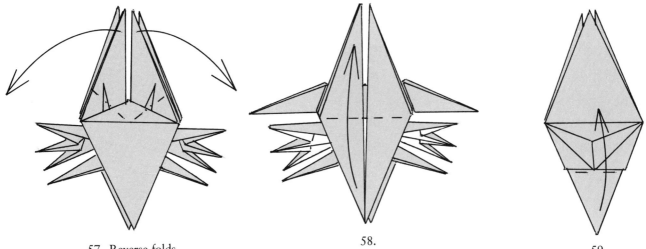

57. Reverse-folds.

58.

59.

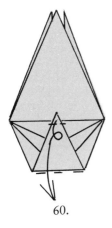

60.

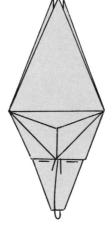

61. Tuck inside.

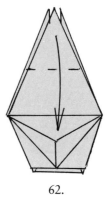

62.

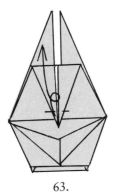

63.

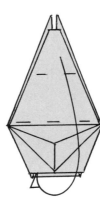

64. Tuck inside.

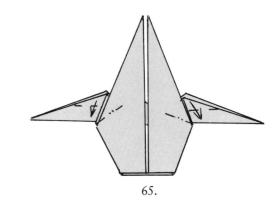

65.

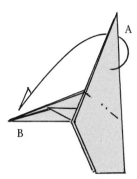

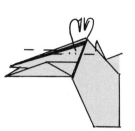

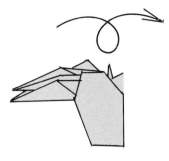

66. Mountain-fold flap A into flap B; repeat on the right.

67. Repeat on the right.

68.

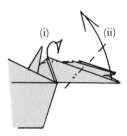

69. (i) Tuck inside.
    (ii) Reverse-fold the pinchers together; repeat on the left side.

70. Open the claw; repeat on the left side.

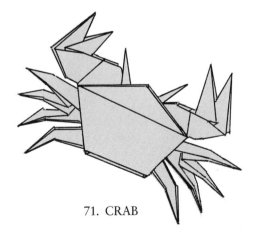

71. CRAB

LOBSTER

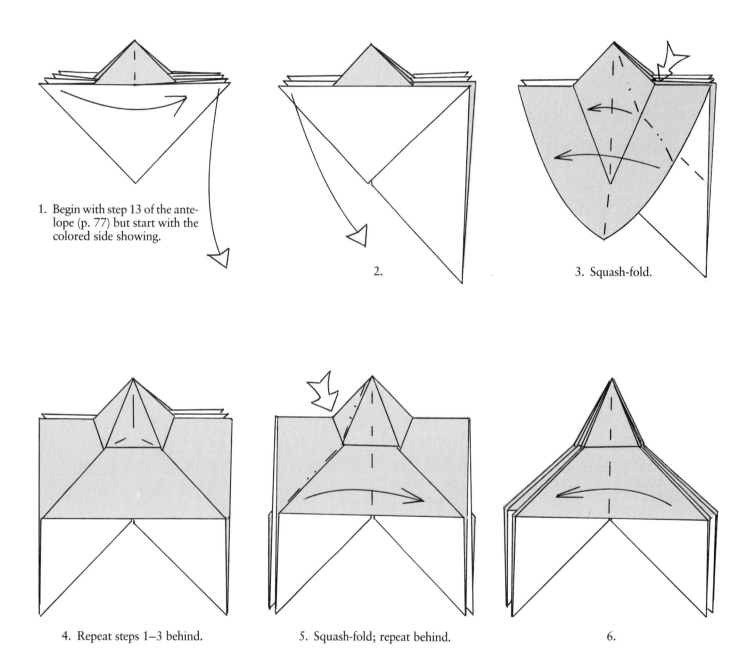

1. Begin with step 13 of the antelope (p. 77) but start with the colored side showing.

2.

3. Squash-fold.

4. Repeat steps 1–3 behind.

5. Squash-fold; repeat behind.

6.

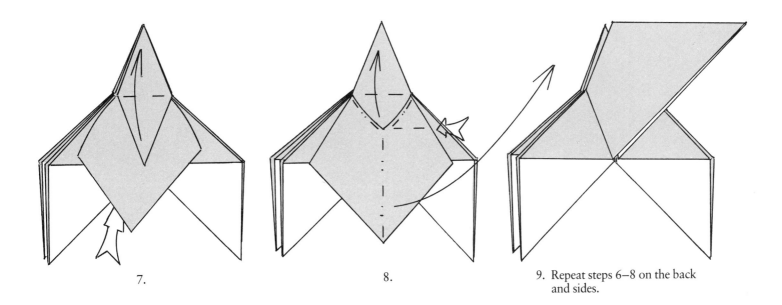

7.

8.

9. Repeat steps 6–8 on the back and sides.

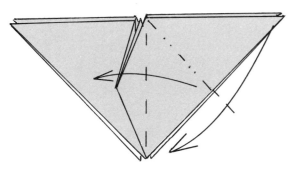

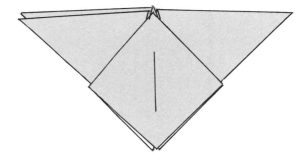

10. Squash-fold.

11. Repeat step 10 on the back and sides.

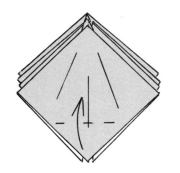

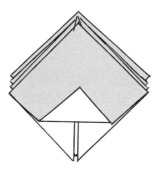

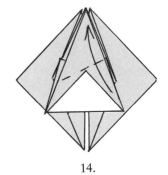

12. Repeat behind.

13. Wing-fold.

14.

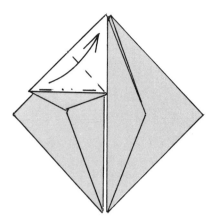

15. Squash-fold.

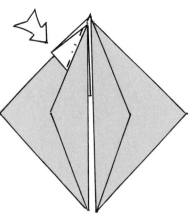

16. Reverse-fold.

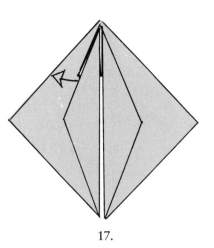

17.

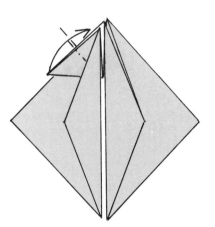

18. Reverse-fold.

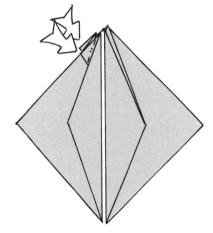

19. Reverse-folds.

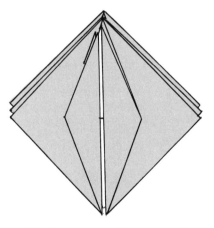

20. Repeat steps 13–19 behind.

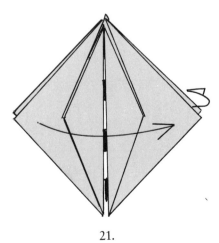

21.

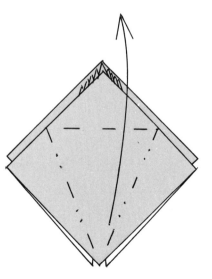

22. Repeat behind.

23. Petal-fold; repeat behind.

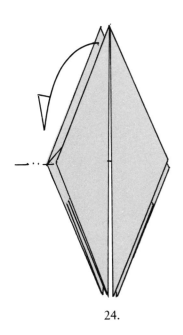

24.

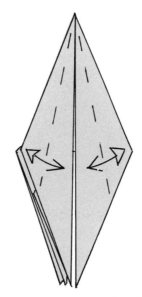

25. This will become the tail.

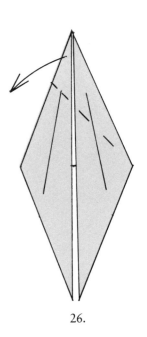

26.

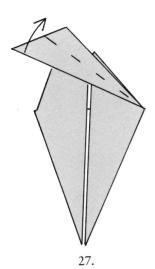

27.

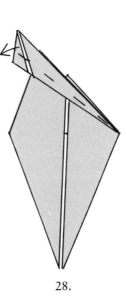

28.

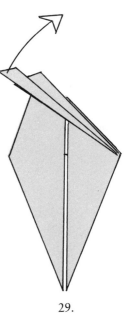

29.

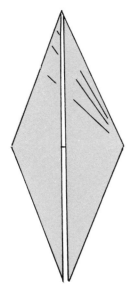

30. Repeat steps 26–29 on the left side.

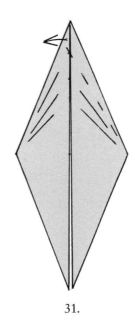

31.

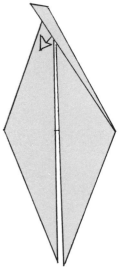

32. Use existing creases to pull out some paper.

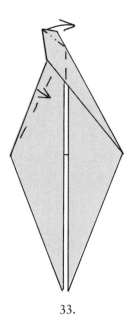

33.

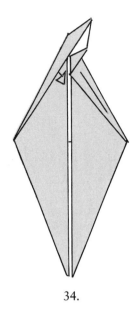

34.

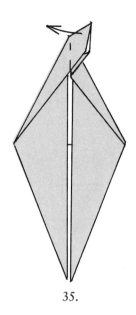

35.

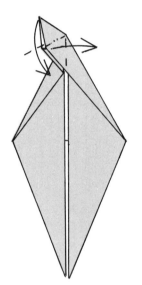

36. Squash-fold.

37.

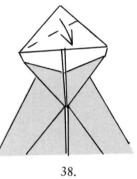

38.

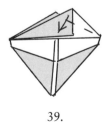

39.

40.

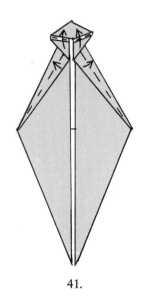

41.

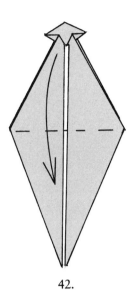

42.

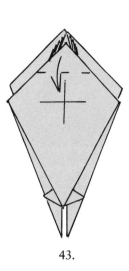

43.

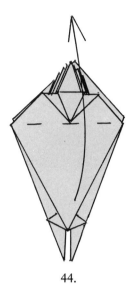

44.

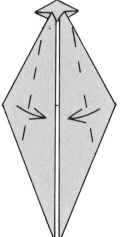

45. Fold on the creases (formed on step 25).

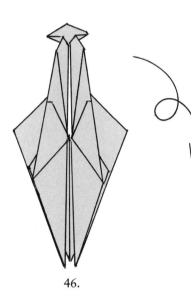

46.

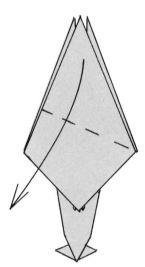

47. This will become the head.

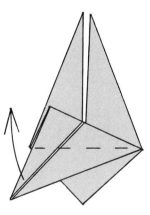

48.

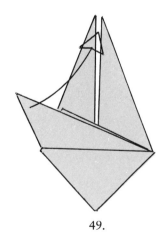

49.

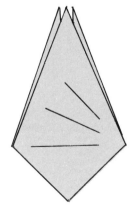

50. Repeat steps 47–49 on the left side.

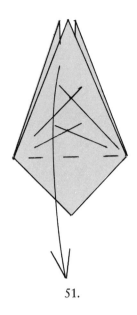

51.

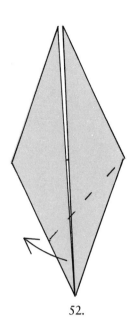

52.

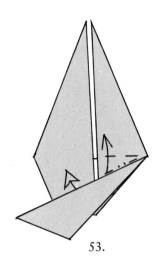

53.

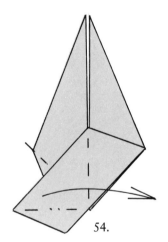

54.

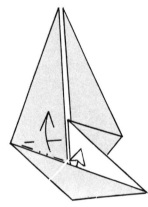

55.

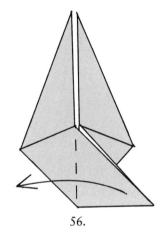

56.

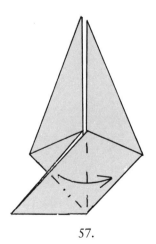

57.

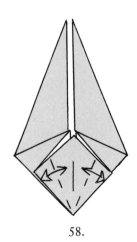

58.

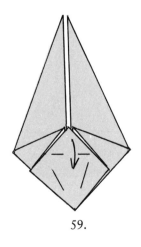

59.

108   ANIMAL ORIGAMI FOR THE ENTHUSIAST

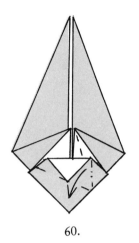

60.

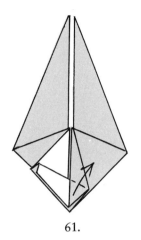

61.

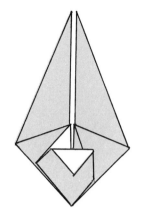

62. Repeat steps 60 & 61 on the
left side.

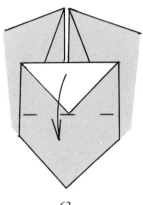

63.

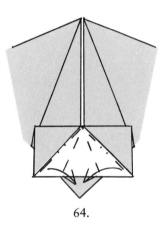

64.

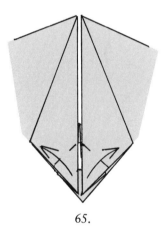

65.

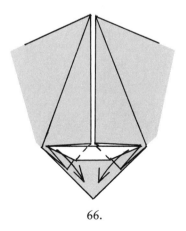

66.

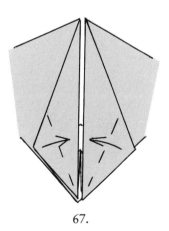

67.

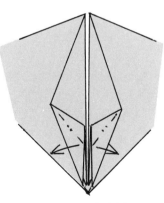

68. Squash-folds.

69. Separate the eyes.

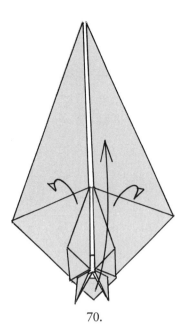

70.

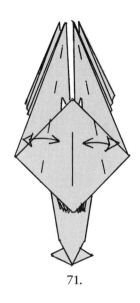

71.

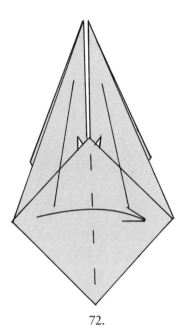

72.

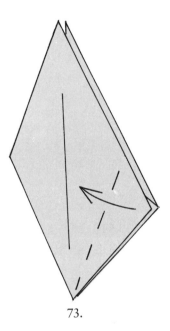

73.

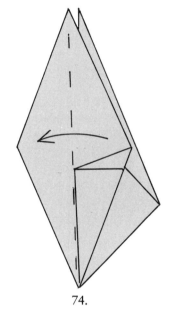

74.

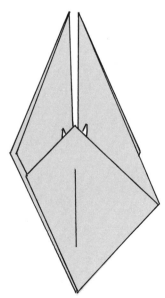

75. Repeat steps 72–74 on the right side.

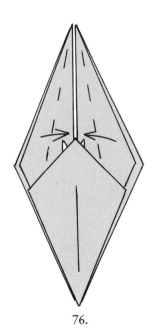

76.

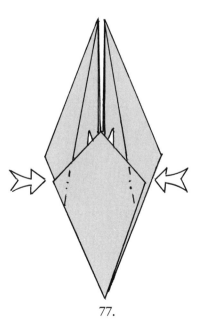

77.

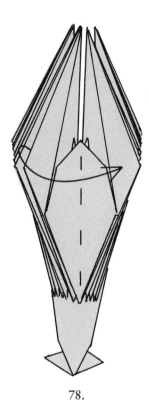

78.

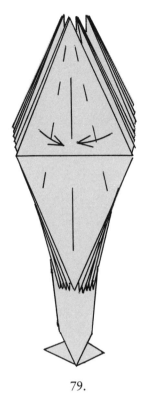

79.

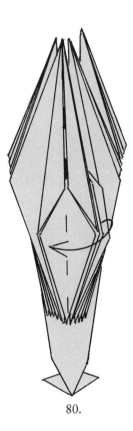

80.

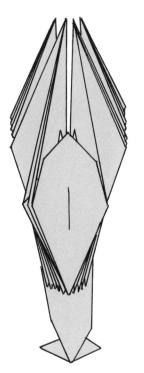

81. Repeat steps 78–80 on the right side.

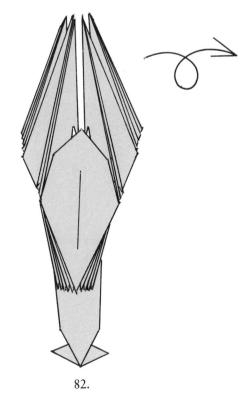

82.

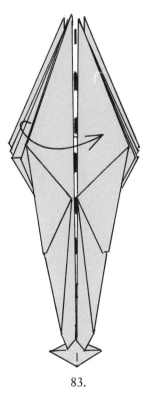

83.

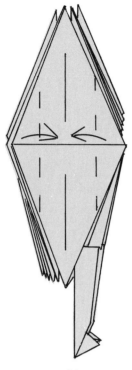

84.

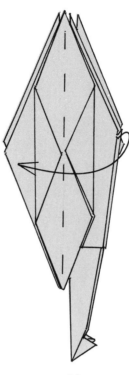

85.

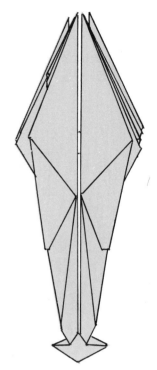

86. Repeat steps 83–85 on the right side.

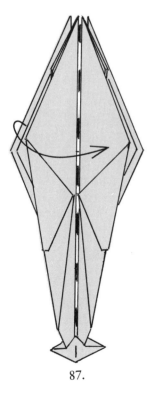

87.

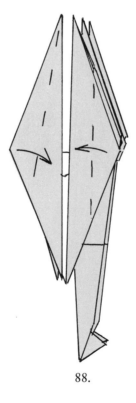

88.

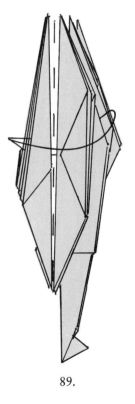

89.

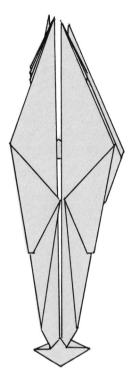

90. Repeat steps 87–89 on the right side.

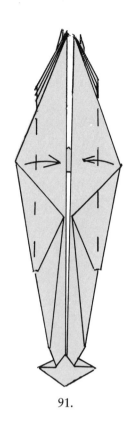

91.

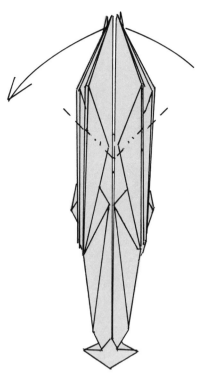

92. Reverse-folds.

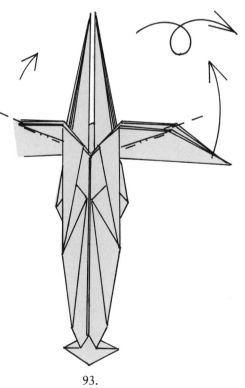

93.

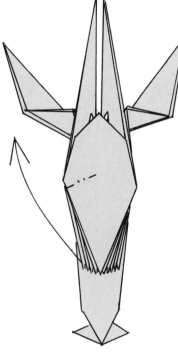

94. Reverse-fold three of the four legs up together.

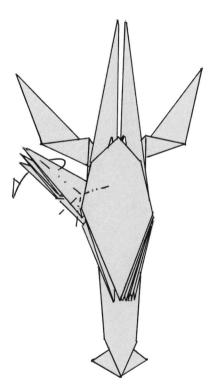

95. Rabbit-ear all the layers together.

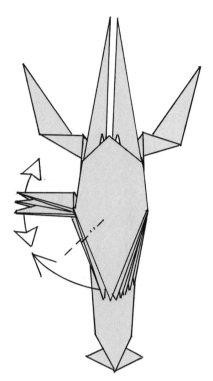

96. Separate the three legs. Reverse-fold the fourth leg.

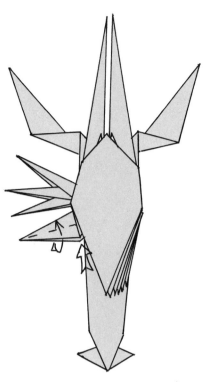

97. Repeat steps 94–97 on the right side.

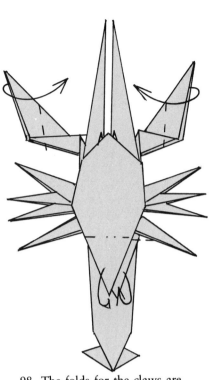

98. The folds for the claws are similar to an outside reverse-fold.

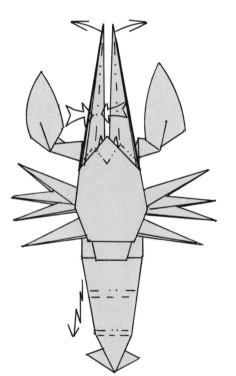

99. Pinch the antennae. Pleat-folds.

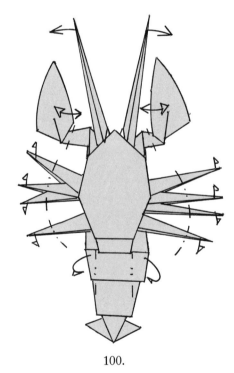

100.

101. LOBSTER

ORNAMENT

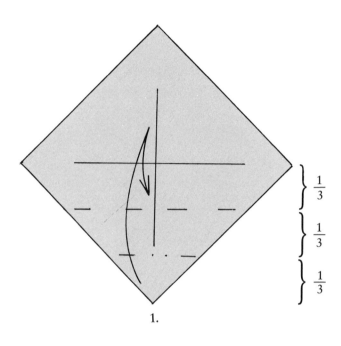

$\frac{1}{3}$

$\frac{1}{3}$

$\frac{1}{3}$

1.

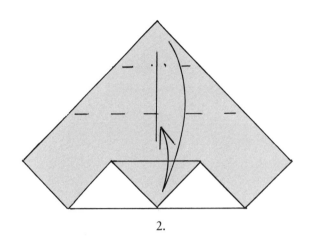

2.

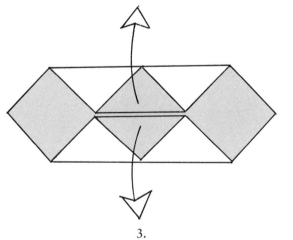

3.

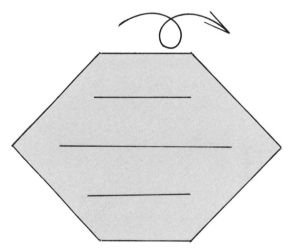

4. Repeat steps 1–3 on the sides.

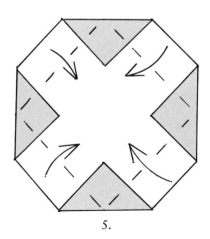

5.

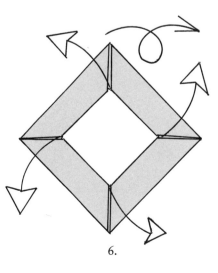

6.

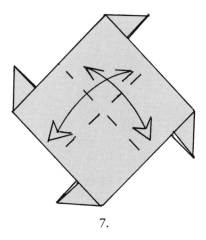

7.

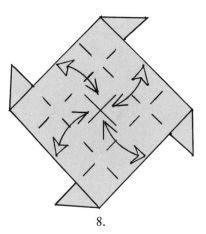

8.

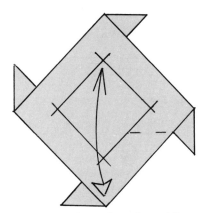

9. Crease only on the indicated line.

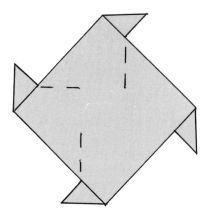

10. Repeat step 9 on the other three sides.

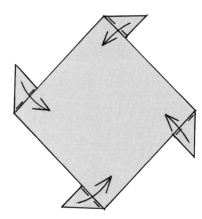

11. Crease sharply.

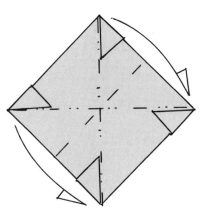

12. Fold the water bomb base.

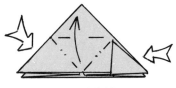

13. Petal-fold.

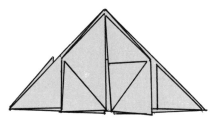

14. Repeat step 13 on the back and sides.

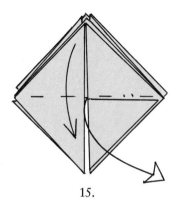

15.

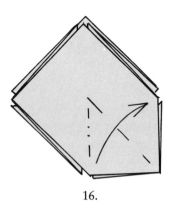

16.

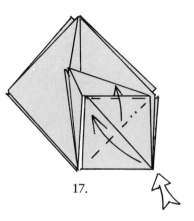

17.

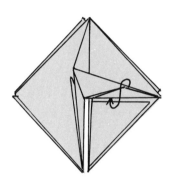

18. Fold inside pocket.

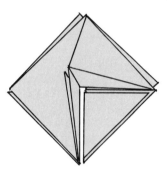

19. Repeat steps 15–18 on the other three sides.

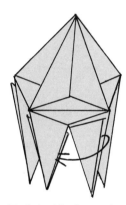

20. Tuck inside the pocket; repeat on the other sides.

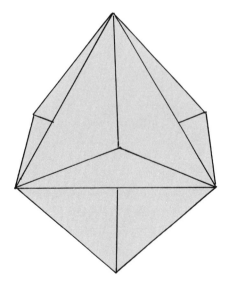

21. ORNAMENT

STAR

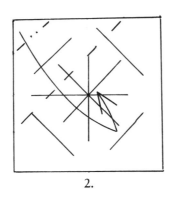

1.

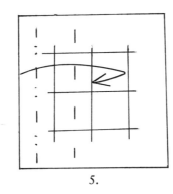

2.

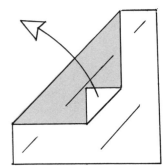

3. Repeat steps 2 & 3 to the other three corners.

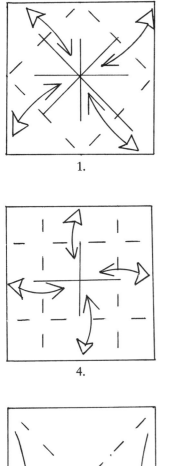

4.

5.

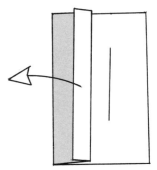

6. Repeat steps 5 & 6 on the other three sides.

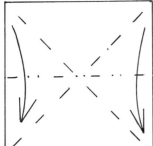

7. Fold the water bomb base.

8. Sink.

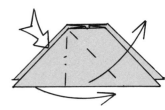

9. Squash-fold.

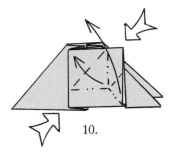

10.

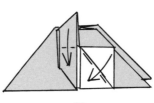

11.

12. Repeat steps 9–11 on the other three sides.

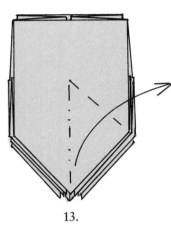

13.

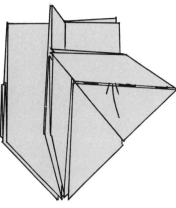

14. Tuck inside.

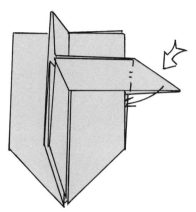

15. Reverse-fold.

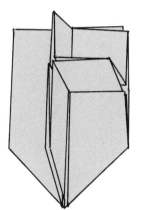

16. Repeat steps 13–15 three times.

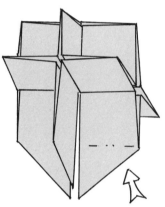

17. Reverse-fold; repeat on the other three sides.

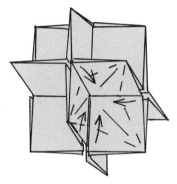

18. Repeat all around.

19. STAR